Overcoming Common Problems

Assertiveness: Step by Step

Dr Windy Dryden and Daniel Constantinou

First published in Great Britain in 2004

Sheldon Press
36 Causton Street
London SW1P 4ST

British Library Cataloguing-in-Publication Data
A catalogue record for this book is available from the British Library

ISBN 978–0–85969–925–9

3 5 7 9 10 8 6 4

Typeset by Deltatype Limited, Birkenhead, Merseyside
First printed and bound in Great Britain by Biddles Ltd
Reprinted and bound in Great Britain by Ashford Colour Press

Produced on paper from sustainable forests

Contents

Daniel dedicates this book to his two beautiful sons
Jordan and Ellis Constantinou

Windy dedicates this book to being childless

Acknowledgements

Daniel wishes to thank Les Seymour for his helpful suggestions and support.

1
What is assertion?

Learning a new language can be very rewarding but is also quite a tough and challenging task. In the same way, training yourself to think, and then speak, in a different way takes real effort and a great deal of practice. When you learn a new language, you may begin by learning simple phrases and then graduate to more complicated sentences in order to engage in conversation. The process at first may be slow and almost mechanical, but with practice you will become more fluent with fewer mistakes.

Learning to be assertive is very similar. It is extremely rewarding to be able to stand up for yourself and no longer be treated like a doormat by other people. Yet familiar communication habits, although unhelpful, are not easy to break. It can be difficult coaching yourself to think and act in a different way. However, although at first it may seem very unnatural, with practice it can become second nature. As we will point out throughout this book, the obstacles to healthy assertion mainly come from ourselves rather than those with whom we are trying to assert ourselves. To paraphrase Shakespeare, 'There is nothing either good or bad, but *rigid, dogmatic* thinking makes it so' (italics ours). As we will point out, our beliefs about ourselves, others and the world in general will have either a positive or a negative impact on our assertion coaching.

In this chapter, we will introduce you to five people who initially found assertion 'impossible', all for different reasons. We will go on to discuss how to become your own assertion coach. We will be looking closely at how to define your behaviour, whether you are acting assertively, aggressively or passively. As you will see, the purpose is different for all three. Chapter 1 will conclude with the general beliefs that underpin assertion, aggression and passivity. Let us now introduce you to five people who are good examples of assertion coaching in action.

The people behind the coaching

The following five individuals are real people who have successfully implemented assertion coaching in their lives. They are from diverse backgrounds and all prevented themselves from being assertive for different reasons. We will use their experiences throughout this book as a means of explaining how you can become your own assertion coach.

1

Denise

Denise is a 46-year-old woman who works as a secretary. Denise decided to have some assertion coaching as she had been experiencing difficulties in her marriage and other significant relationships. She explained that everyone 'put on her', from her daughter to her best friend. They all seemed to use her, with little, if any, gratitude in return. Denise believed that she could never say 'no' to others' requests as she would experience too much guilt. Denise also explained that her mother still treated her like a little girl, expecting Denise to do exactly what she told her to do.

Joan

Joan is a 53-year-old woman who is a very successful investment banker. She had been struggling with alcohol dependence for some time and described herself as a very nervous person who was fearful of confrontation. Joan's main issue centred on her relationship with her husband. He had a habit of minimizing her achievements in life, and claiming that it was his influence that led to her success. He took delight in putting her down while in the company of their friends. Joan was so scared of being rejected that she never stood up for herself. She explained that her husband dominated her and that she used alcohol as a way of escaping the relationship problem.

Colin

Colin is a 37-year-old man who is managing director of his own firm. Colin realized that throughout his life he had never been treated with any regard at all. He explained that his experience was that people treated him unfairly, and his friends just wanted to get what they could out of him. He found it hard to recount any occasion where he stood up for himself. This was because he believed that assertion was not kind and decent. He demanded of himself that he never hurt others, and simply believed that others should naturally be honest and respectable without his having to assert himself in any way.

John

John is a 31-year-old man who works as a stockbroker. John found that he had a very short temper with people, and that while his anger was effective in getting people to do things for him, it was detrimental to his intimate relationships. John explained that he wanted to be able to get closer to people, especially his girlfriend, who found his angry outbursts very difficult to handle. John explained that his girlfriend had threatened to leave if he did not find some way to 'control' his anger. John had also occasionally hit out at inanimate objects during arguments with his girlfriend.

George

Finally, let us introduce you to George, a 33-year-old man who works as a carpenter. George firmly believed that his family, particularly his father, would only contact him when they wanted something. Although he was very angry about this, George would never say anything to his father or his family. He believed that his feelings were best kept to himself. This, he assumed, kept him in control and helped him avoid hurting anyone with what he could say. As a result he allowed issues to build up. On the rare occasions that he did pipe up, his family discredited what he was saying as George seemed to be 'over-emotional'. George described himself as a very sensitive person, who felt deeply for others but found it very hard to express this. He also had some fundamental issues from his childhood that he wished to discuss with his parents, but refrained from doing so because he feared their response.

We will be using Denise, Joan, Colin, John and George's experiences with assertion coaching throughout this book to show how they put assertion into practice in their lives. Before that we will define exactly what assertion is and what it isn't.

The nature and purpose of assertion

The dictionary defines assertion as a declaration of truth, an affirmation and an appropriate insistence upon a right. Assertion is the honest communication of our emotions in a way that does not abuse others. The nature of assertion is that we can state a preference very strongly without insisting that another must see it our way. As we will point out, the nature of assertion is multi-faceted, but a succinct definition is as follows:

> Assertion is the flexible pursuit of having our preferences met, our opinions voiced, our emotions and beliefs honestly communicated in an appropriate way at the relevant time.

The purpose of assertion is to create and maintain a realistic view of our worth as an individual living in a community. The intention of assertion is not for us to act in a superior way to others, but to accept that we are all equal in worth. This means that we are all just as deserving as one another in having our preferences met. Consequently, the nature of assertion is not a hedonistic pursuit of what we want to the constant detriment of others. On the other hand, the goal of assertion is not to be constantly serving other people either. Assertion is not intended to encourage you to engage in behaviour that indicates that others are better or more deserving than you are. The purpose of assertion involves standing up for your own wishes, wants and desires but taking into account that those of others may be of equal importance. The purpose of assertion is not to win arguments but to agree on a workable compromise. When we are being truly assertive, it is with the purpose of ideally satisfying the preferences of both parties involved in a situation.

We will now consider why assertion is far healthier and more practical than aggression or passivity. We will do this by defining aggression and passivity, including a description of the purpose of all three.

Assertion, aggression and passivity and the purpose of all three

In this section, we will show how assertion is distinctly different from aggression and passivity. First, let us define what we mean by aggression.

Aggression may be defined as an approach to communication which is mainly hostile, forceful or bullying. Aggression does mean standing up for oneself, but with little if any regard for others. Someone who is aggressive instead of assertive would be dismissive of the preferences or emotions of others and certainly not willing to work on a balanced compromise. Aggression only allows for an expression of one's own preferences, seeing others' contributions as being of less importance, inferior or even meaningless.

The purpose of aggression is vastly different from assertion or passivity as it is all about winning, or getting your own way to the detriment of others. The intended result of aggression is to 'get them before they get you', and continually acting aggressively reinforces this unhealthy philosophy. That is why John, introduced earlier, found his aggression so useful. It seemed to give him an immediate short-term reward of getting what he wanted. In his job as a stockbroker he would aggressively dismiss or belittle others' preferences and only value and enforce his own opinion. John believed this gave him power over others, and that he could get them to do exactly what he wanted.

John also found that he would sometimes experience temper tantrums to reduce pent-up aggression. When these were focused on one of his subordinates he would excuse his behaviour by saying, 'They had it coming to them,' or 'Who do they think they are to talk to me like that?' Making excuses and blaming others for aggressive outbursts are very common traits in people who use aggression when communicating. The reason for this is that they do not take responsibility for their own emotions but would rather blame others for obstructing their desired goals.

Along with the immediate gratification that goes with aggression, there is also the praise from onlookers. Others can reinforce the rewards of aggression by praising you, admiring your seeming healthy modus operandi. John explained that on many occasions members of his team would commend him for ripping into someone who 'crossed' him. For example, they would say, 'I wish I could speak to people like that,' or 'You certainly showed him who's the boss.' This all fed into a very unhealthy view that others were there primarily to serve him, and that his preferences had to come first before all others.

Another characteristic of aggression is that you state your opinions as facts, and sarcastically put others' opinions down. This too is wearing over time, because expressing your opinion as a fact does not teach others to hone their own ability to evaluate situations. If others believe your sarcasm, they will find it increasingly more difficult to come up with realistic solutions to their problems. Over time, expressing your opinions as facts will foster an over-dependency from others. They will buy into the view that you are an all-knowing, all-wise guru who must be consulted before they make any important decisions. This may lead to further frustration as others attempt to drain your resources with their problems.

The immediate pay-offs of getting others to jump when you say jump may seem very appealing, but aggression does have long-term drawbacks. It is the purpose of aggression to keep you in a state of alert to be prepared for any possible 'attack' from others. You may be protecting yourself, but it will consequently be a great drain on your energy because you will constantly have to remain vigilant for the next attack. Aggression over time can also cultivate mistrust for people and this lack of trust can feed back on your intimate relationships. You may also feel guilt or shame when reflecting on past aggressive behaviour. While experiencing the guilt and shame, you may engage in apologetic over-helpful behaviours in an attempt to nullify or right the aggressive episode.

This was John's experience. He found the short-term comforts and seemingly immediate rewards of aggression very appealing. The effects on the recipients of his aggression were usually fear, anxiety or counter-aggression. These responses led to individuals around John working against him rather than with him. His aggression also triggered

5

disinclination from the recipient to be helpful to John in the future. John also observed that his girlfriend lived in fear of his aggression: although doing what he told her, she resented him and their relationship was deteriorating as a result. In short, John's aggressive communication style was creating enemies for him. Consequently this confirmed the unhealthy idea that he must always be alert and vigilant around other people, creating a vicious cycle that he believed was impossible to break.

In summary, the purpose of aggression is to promote and maintain the idea that you are superior or more important in all or many respects. Although in the short term aggression seems to work, the long-term effect on you and others is very detrimental. Others may carry out your requests through fear, but will eventually resent you for it. Aggression in the long term leaves you at risk of an unhealthy view of yourself and others; you will be unable to relax in their company, and consequently all your relationships will be tense.

Passivity is simply the opposite of the above. Passivity can be defined as a lack of initiative or force, or continually being submissive. Passivity means avoiding standing up for oneself, and giving too much regard to the opinion and preferences of others. This was exactly what Denise experienced when she expressed her preferences and emotions. She voiced her wishes so weakly that others easily dismissed them, or missed them altogether. She found that she would also answer personal questions with dishonest statements that did not truly represent what she actually believed or felt. She would attempt to assume how others wanted her to converse or behave, and then adapt her conversation or behaviour accordingly, even if this was to her detriment.

For example, she would be asked to care for her friend's children while her friend went shopping. On being asked if that was an inconvenience, Denise would always automatically answer, 'It's no problem, I don't mind in the slightest,' although this could not be further from the truth. She would keep her true opinion quiet, 'just in case' her friend took offence or felt hurt at her response. This is highly characteristic of passivity, as you denigrate your opinion or contribution and over-value the opinions and contributions of others. Passive behaviour encourages the belief that others are superior and what they believe or have to offer is more meaningful and far more important than what you have to offer.

One of the main purposes of passivity is to avoid the discomfort of conflict and continue to please others at your own expense. Acting passively means that you get an immediate reduction in anxiety, because the threat of standing up for yourself has been temporarily avoided. Apart from the temporary reduction in anxiety, passivity also allows you to avoid feeling guilty when you sense that by being assertive you may upset someone. The purpose of passivity, like aggression, is to give immediate satisfaction, although the longer-term effects may lead to greater passive behaviour.

For example, Colin the managing director would always pay his staff a full day's pay even when he knew they had actually only worked half-days, leaving the workplace early to go home. Colin would avoid any possible confrontation with his staff, which meant that he received an instant pay-off because his anxiety immediately subsided as the threat seemed to go away. Yet this was only a short-term solution: inevitably he would be faced with a similar situation as they knew they could get away with it and still be paid. Both Denise and Colin used their passive communication style to avoid the discomfort of assertion, choosing the quickest route to what seemed an easy life. By relying on the short-term solution of passivity, they were unable to learn to address any situations healthily, and hence their preferences were seldom met.

Passivity also promotes the unrealistic notion that others have poor resources to handle disappointment or frustrations. When acting passively you assume that it is you who would be completely responsible for hurting someone's feelings, and do not consider that other people largely have control of their own emotions. This is what stopped George from being assertive with his family, especially his father. He feared that they couldn't cope with him speaking his mind. He rationalized this by saying, 'They should already know what I want without me having to spell it out for them.'

Another problem perpetuated by frequent passivity is the development and maintenance of unhealthy beliefs about yourself and your worth. Acting passively reinforces the irrational belief that others are more worthy, more intelligent or superior to you. That is why Denise and Colin allowed people, significant and non-significant, to walk all over them and treat them like a doormat. By allowing people to repeatedly walk all over them they lost most of their self-confidence. Over time they developed an even lower opinion about themselves, believing they did not have the capability to stand up for themselves.

For example, after years of passivity Denise had come to the conclusion that 'I am unable to change, because others are so much stronger than I am', and Colin falsely reasoned, 'I just can't assert myself, I am just not made that way.' Years of passivity had encouraged them to behave in a way that promoted the unhealthy idea that they were there to be used. Their lack of assertion also taught others that they could be used, and in some cases even controlled. This was Joan's experience, as her husband capitalized on her passive communication style and controlled her to his own gain. At first it triggered thoughts of pity from her friends who witnessed or heard about his behaviour. Some of Joan's friends even praised her for her unselfish self-sacrificing nature. Joan also found that some close friends attempted to rescue her from her seemingly helpless, powerless passive state. Over time, though, her passivity became increasingly irritating and frustrating for others and eventually switched people off altogether, with some of them distancing themselves from her. Joan experienced a loss of respect and approval from her friends, the one thing she was working so passively for.

The immediate pay-off for passivity seems very appealing. To begin with you avoid any discomfort and seem to be pleasing others and making life easier for all concerned. The costs are that in the long run it is usually to your detriment. Although initially passivity seems to be the best option, after a period of time you lose your sense of identity, your self-confidence and the one thing you have been trying to earn – respect and approval from others.

Summary

It should be clear, after considering the above, that the nature and purpose of assertion, aggression and passivity are all distinctly different. We will briefly define assertion, aggression and passivity, and then compare all three.

As already mentioned, the purpose of *assertion* is the flexible pursuit of getting our preferences met, our opinions voiced and our emotions and beliefs honestly communicated in an appropriate way. The purpose of *aggression* is different altogether, as it is all about winning, or getting your own way, to the detriment of others. The purpose of *passivity* is to avoid the discomfort of conflict, and to continue to please others at your own expense.

Contrasting assertion with aggression and passivity

We will now highlight four ways that assertion is distinctly different from aggression and passivity.

Assertion promotes a healthy view of self

Assertion contrasts with aggression and passivity as it promotes a healthy view of self, a sense of equal value and self-worth. It does not advocate, as does aggression, that you are more important and hence should be given special attention. Nor does it advocate the passive position that you are worth less than others. The human equality advocated by assertion is beneficial as it is a more accurate and realistic appraisal of human worth. Realistically your preferences will not always be met because you share this planet with billions of other equal human beings with their own opinions and preferences. Assertion will help you experience and overcome the disappointments at these times far more quickly.

In direct comparison, when your preferences are not met, aggression will dictate that you become more aggressive or vindictive in your behaviour. This will lead to tension, more enemies being made and rash decisions taken. Passivity, on the other hand, would have you accept this as more evidence of your helpless plight in life. This will lead to less communication, more life dissatisfaction, and more bowing and scraping to others' needs. Assertion is far healthier than aggression and passivity as it keeps you focused on communicating honestly your thoughts and feelings, thus strengthening your healthy sense of self. Assertion also keeps you more accepting of others as equally deserving. This means that you will face the disappointment of not having your preferences met more quickly and healthily.

Assertion promotes a healthy view of others

Assertion contrasts with aggression and passivity as it promotes a healthy view of others, rather than viewing them as a threat. Assertion promotes acceptance of others' capabilities and encourages a healthy alliance where you can work together utilizing each other's strengths. Aggression, in comparison, advocates that you must be ever vigilant of others, and wherever possible control them before they control you. Indeed, your aggression may well lead people to feel resentful towards you, and then people will work against you rather than with you. Passivity contrasts with assertion and aggression in that there is often an assumption that others are more important than you and therefore must be served and revered. With passivity you esteem others too highly and expect far too much from them; this ultimately leads to your experiencing unhealthy emotions when you infer that you have been let down.

Assertion also contrasts with aggression and passivity by implying that others are responsible for their own emotions. This leads to healthy honest communication that respects others' capability to handle their own disappointments without your trying to protect them from it. Aggression, on the other hand, gives off the message that 'my opinions are all that matter, and you are far less important than me'. This is an unhealthy view of others. Passivity, in contrast, takes all the responsibility for others' emotions. Passivity advocates that you can directly hurt others, so you must be kind and thoughtful by not burdening them with your preferences. Passivity assumes that it is better if you go without rather than troubling or perhaps offending an individual.

In summary, we believe that assertion is far healthier than aggression and passivity as it reinforces a healthy respect and evaluation of others.

Assertion will construct healthy respectful relationships where your preferences and those of others will be appropriately met.

Assertion reinforces your sense of identity and self-confidence

In contrast with aggression and passivity, assertion promotes your sense of identity and self-confidence, making your view known even when it may not be regarded. Although your preference may not be met, the important aspect is that you voice your opinion. By doing so you maintain your self-confidence and learn to believe in yourself and your ability. Assertion stops you from obsessively going over and over what you believe you should or should not have said at that particular time. By not doing this you will lessen your vulnerability to putting yourself down and this will maintain your self-confidence.

Assertion promotes and maintains a clear sense of your identity, encouraging ongoing communication of what you like and what you do not like. This keeps you focused on what your preferences actually are. Aggression, in contrast to assertion and passivity, encourages an exaggerated sense of identity where only you are important. This would be perfectly acceptable if you were the only human alive. Passivity, on the other hand, encourages you to hold back from asserting your preference. After some time you will lose focus on what it is you used to believe or like doing. This relinquishing of your preference over time lessens your sense of identity. That is why I (WD) encourage appropriate disagreement as it is the royal road to self-identity.

In summary, we believe assertion is far healthier than aggression and passivity as it reinforces your sense of identity by keeping your preferences to the fore. Assertion also contrasts with aggression and passivity as it produces and maintains your self-confidence in handling difficult situations without passively giving in to the other person, or becoming uncontrollably aggressive.

Assertion saves time and energy

In contrast to aggression and passivity, assertion saves you time and energy. By being assertive you will be partaking in open, honest communication. This saves time, as you will not need to rely on others guessing exactly what your preferences are. Assertion also saves you energy as you are not so stressed and tense, always anticipating an attack. If you are passive you will spend large amounts of time pleasing others so as not to offend or hurt them. Passivity also costs you as it takes great energy repressing and holding back your opinions, preferences and feelings. Eventually, though, your energy will weaken in your passive resolve, and you will erupt in an aggressive outburst.

The reason for this unhealthy eruption is because passivity will not always help you to repress your feelings in front of others. Eventually someone or something will trigger you off, and then suddenly, without restraint, you display unhealthy emotions that others will see as completely 'over the top' for the situation. At this point accusatory and derogatory statements flood out of you in an uncontrolled, unproductive way. This passive-to-aggressive swing will use up huge amounts of energy. Then time will be required to patch up your unhealthy outburst, passively giving in to over-helpful apologetic behaviours. This is why I (DC) encourage clients to 'beware of the fury of the passive person'.

In contrast with passivity and aggression, assertion advocates early intervention and an offloading or sharing of opinions over time. Assertion lowers the risk of over-energetic unhealthy aggressive outbursts and 'end of your tether' name-calling, such as 'That's it, I've had it with you, you useless idiot.'

In summary, we believe assertion is a far healthier option than aggression and passivity as it advocates early intervention that counteracts unhealthy time-wasting behaviour. Assertion contrasts with aggression and passivity as it advocates open, honest communication, saving you time, as the other party knows exactly what your preference is. Assertion also saves energy as it advocates consistent communication of opinions, and this process counteracts unhealthy outbursts.

How to identify whether you are being assertive, aggressive or passive

We have not yet encountered any individual who is perfectly assertive all the time. It is therefore important to identify clearly what particular mode of communication you are employing. If you are healthily asserting yourself, it will be evident by the particular terms you are using. Assertion will also be evident by the modulation in your speech tone and by your body language. It is also important to be able to recognize whether you are being assertive, aggressive or passive as initial attempts at assertion are usually unsophisticated and need refinement. Assertion coaching at first requires you to be objective in your self-analysis so as to be able to refine your new skill. That is why the following behavioural characteristics are important: they serve to help you analyse, identify and modify your initial attempts at assertion.

A cautionary note

Avoid putting yourself down if you find that you started assertively but seem to end up being either passive or aggressive. Falling back into passivity or aggression is a common experience for most individuals learning to become assertive. The reason for this falling back is that aggression or passivity may seem more comfortable and/or familiar to you. You have practised it so much more and hence are used to it. It has also been the experience of some that they may over-compensate by swinging from previously being passively meek and mild to being demanding and aggressive, or of course vice versa.

Rest assured that this oscillation is a common occurrence, but it needs addressing, for left unchecked it can become very unhealthy. It is unhealthy because the purpose of assertion is to redress the balance in your life, not to keep you being passive in one situation and aggressive in another. Do not be disheartened, then, with your initial attempts at assertion. As our illustration at the beginning of the chapter pointed out, assertion is much like learning a new language. At first it seems foreign and unnatural, but with practice your mistakes will become minimal. Keep up your healthy resolve and keep learning from your mistakes.

The following will aid you in identifying whether you are behaving assertively, aggressively or passively. We will initially specify the behaviour associated with assertion, outlining at first the particular terms you would use to express yourself, then the modulation in your voice and finally the body language associated with assertion.

Identifying assertion

As already stated, assertion is a flexible pursuit of our preferences, communicating our emotions and beliefs in an honest, appropriate way, while respecting others' boundaries. The terms we choose to use when asserting ourselves can have either a beneficial or a detrimental effect. The list below summarizes a few of these. These statements add weight to your assertion coaching and will work to increase the chances of your preferences being met. The list can also aid you in identifying which mode of communication you are using. Identifying whether you are being assertive is essential so that you can hone your assertion skills. An objective review of your initial attempts at assertion and a correcting of your mistakes will be a catalyst to healthy change. We will now highlight the particular terms that are commonly associated with assertion. When being assertive your communication is character-ized by:

'I' statements
'I' statements are specific, brief and easily understood, such as:

> 'I prefer to ...'
> 'I would like to ...'
> 'I do not agree that ...'
> 'I feel disappointed when ...'

These 'I' statements make clear what you think and feel about a particular point. They are focused, succinct and clear, rather than vague and rambling. This enables your hearer to know exactly what it is that you are asserting. 'I' statements are to the point, and are hence easily understood by others. They are healthy as they assume personal responsibility, not attempting to diffuse responsibility with some ominous third party, i.e. 'We think you had better . . .'

Distinguishing between fact and opinion

Distinguishing between fact and opinion is healthy as it removes bigotry. Your opinion is not the only one. This distinction reinforces the healthy idea that life consists of shades of grey and is not just black or white. When asserting yourself you would express your opinions using the following:

'In my opinion . . .'
'As I understand it . . .'
'My experience is different to that . . .'

These statements accept the scope for others' opinions but clearly assert your own. They are not dismissive but realistically accept that your way is not the only way of doing things.

Enquiring of others' preferences and opinions

Enquiring of others' preferences and opinions follows from our last point as it maintains a healthy realistic view of yourself, others and the world. Assertion allows and encourages open discussion of others' preferences and opinions. For example, when enquiring of others you make use of the following questions:

'What are your thoughts on . . .?'
'What suggestions do you have on overcoming . . .?'
'How does that fit in with you?'

These questions open up discussion, giving others the opportunity to assert their preferences. For this reason, assertion avoids closed 'leading' statements such as 'You don't mind, do you?' Actually, assertion encourages an exploration of others' opinions, suggestions and solutions. For example, in a discussion you may say directly: 'I am finding it difficult to come up with a solution here. How would you suggest we tackle this problem?' This again reinforces the healthy belief that you are not the only one with good ideas and solutions. In our personal experience, making these enquiries has yielded new innovative approaches that we would perhaps not have come up with otherwise.

Constructive criticism without dogmatic suggestion

Assertion encourages you to offer constructive criticism without dogmatically telling the other person or group what to do. For example, when offering constructive criticism you may employ the following:

13

'I feel disappointed when you ...'
'I find it unacceptable when you ...'
'I have noticed recently that ... [stating specific behaviour]'

This constructive criticism is not an attack on the other person as a whole. Unlike aggression, assertion does not endeavour to assassinate the entire character of an individual. This constructive criticism is specific and aims to give feedback enabling the other person to understand the impact their behaviour has on you. It is not out to demoralize or purposely hurt others, although they may end up by hurting themselves about what you have said because of the unhealthy beliefs that they hold about your assertion. Its main purpose is to highlight your thoughts and feelings about their behaviour, and give them an accurate appraisal of how you feel about it.

If appropriate, this feedback could be followed up with a suggestion of a more preferable approach, for example:

'How about trying it this way ...?'
'It may benefit you to ...'
'Would you find it more helpful if ...?'

These non-dogmatic flexible suggestions give the individual the respect and dignity to make their own choice. This will encourage others to want to engage in your preference willingly rather than grudgingly, which means that they are more likely to accept your feedback and suggestion. This hopefully in turn would mean that they will apply your suggestion for a longer period of time than if they thought you enforced your preference on them aggressively.

With assertion, it is not only what we say that has an impact, but also how we say it. How we express ourselves can work for or against us. We will now draw attention to particular vocal tones and speech patterns commonly associated with assertion. When being assertive you probably would utilize the following.

A steady, warm vocal tone
A steady, warm tone is a mark of an individual who is confident about what he or she is saying. When being assertive you will give warmth in the relevant places, emphasizing the key words you are stressing. This warmth will give your listener a clearer understanding of the thoughts you are conveying.

Vocal volume to fit surroundings
When asserting yourself your vocal tone would ideally be loud enough for your listener not to have to strain to catch what you are saying. On the other hand, your volume would not be too loud, as this could irritate

14

or overwhelm your listener. When being assertive you would vary your modulation and volume on key words as this highlights your point, giving weight to the possibility of a favourable outcome.

Fluent speech pattern with a steady pace

Fluency is thoughtful speech that flows with ease and freedom. When being assertive you would clearly express your opinion or your preference without unnatural hesitancy and stumbling. Your fluent steady tone gives the message of inner conviction and a certainty in what you are asserting. Obviously no one can maintain word-perfect assertion, although sentence fillers such as 'er' and 'um' would, ideally, be kept to a minimum if not eliminated altogether. A steady, firm voice with few hesitations and an even pace is a hallmark of competent assertion coaching.

It is commonly accepted that a large percentage of our communication is non-verbal. For our assertion to be effective, it is beneficial to back it up with healthy body language. Our posture and gestures can either reinforce or undermine the pursuit of getting our preferences met. We will now focus on the body language commonly associated with assertion. When being assertive you probably would display the following.

Maintaining eye contact

Eye contact that is firm but not overbearing is a very important feature of assertion. This is not a staring out, or glaring, but an eye-to-eye focus which is inviting. As we will go on to point out in 'Identifying passivity' (see p. 20), looking down or away denotes shame or a lack of confidence. Maintaining good consistent eye contact communicates a message of faith and confidence in what you are asserting.

Appropriate facial expressions

When being assertive your facial expressions will be congruent with how you are feeling at that particular time. For example, when pleased you would smile appropriately; when frustrated, perhaps you would frown. In being assertive, though, your facial features would generally be consistent with the message you are conveying. Appropriate facial expressions would also be evident by your facial muscles. These would feel and look relaxed, not twitchy or shaky.

Inviting body movement and posture

While being assertive your body movement would be inviting, not closed or protective. For example, while being assertive you may gesture with open hand movements, doing so in a rhythmical fashion.

You would not be jerky or stilted, nor gesture by pointing your finger or shaking your fist. Furthermore, your arms would not be folded, as this is defensive and not assertive.

Your posture when being assertive would again be relaxed and confident. You would not be slouched in a nonchalant fashion, or bolt upright looking uncomfortably tense.

Your standing or sitting position when being assertive would also reflect those with whom you are being assertive. For example, if the individual you are being assertive with were sitting, then you would not stand over them, as this can appear menacing and aggressive. In addition, you preferably would not allow the other person to stand over you, as this could foster a sense of superiority on their part. The ideal assertive position is having both you and the other party standing or sitting at the same level.

We have discussed speech, vocal tones and body language that would indicate that you are being assertive. We will now highlight how you can identify when you are being aggressive.

Identifying aggression

As mentioned already, aggression is all about winning, or getting your own way to the detriment of others. We will now highlight the particular terms that are commonly associated with aggression. This list is to serve as a framework for you to identify whether you are being aggressive. When being aggressive you would probably make use of the following terms:

Prominent 'I' statements

With aggression, you would be stressing your opinion and yours alone. Prominent 'I' statements leave little, if any, room for others' view or challenges. For example:

'*I* must have . . .'
'*I* think . . .'
'*My* view is . . .'

These forms of 'I' statements go to back up the unhealthy view that you are superior in acumen or decision-making or are just better all round compared to other people. That is why the prominent 'I' statements are usually backed up with boastful 'I am better than you' statements. For example, after aggressively declaring an 'I' statement, you may also add:

'and I am never wrong,'

or

'I saw that coming, and I told you so,'

or even, perhaps,

'I would never let this get on top of me.'

These boastful remarks tacked on to the end of a prominent 'I' statement will go to fuel the unhealthy idea that you are superior to others. This in turn fuels further aggression and will keep you dissatisfied and uneasy in your relationships with others.

No distinction between fact and your opinion
When being aggressive you would express your opinions as facts. There would be no grey area, but only black or white. While being aggressive, then, you would express your opinions probably using the following terms:

'What we are going to do is ...'
'No, no, the way to do it is ...'
'You've not used your brain, that's completely useless ...'

These statements dismiss others' preferences and opinions and go to reinforce your own. Aggressively enforcing your opinions as facts intends to put the other person or group down, for you enforce your suggestion as the only way. This aggressive approach can seem very successful. The reason for this success is that often people accept your opinion because you seem so sure. You may have also noted that the above examples have a sarcastic tone. This follows, as when you are being aggressive you are more prone to sarcasm. Sarcasm adds weight to dismissing others' views and belittling their suggestions. This again fosters an unhealthy view of your value and ability, which can eventually become very tiresome to maintain.

Enquiries and requests that provoke fear
Aggression uses fear as a means of getting your preferences carried out or your ideas accepted. For this reason, when making an enquiry you might employ the following questions:

'What do you think you are doing?'
'Haven't you finished yet?'

This aggressive form of questioning is aimed at triggering off fear in the recipient so as to get a quick response to your request. This line of enquiry is often backed up with threatening consequences, for example:

'You had better get that done immediately, or else ...'
'If you do not go and do what I have asked you now ...'

The main purpose of these fear-provoking enquiries and requests is to control the behaviour of another. It is not the intention of this aggressive approach to allow others the opportunity to make their own minds up on the matter.

Manipulative advice-giving

Manipulative advice-giving is also aggressive. It is aggressive because it engenders the unhealthy idea that others are less able to make good decisions, and that you can control or manipulate them to your own ends. When giving advice aggressively you may use the following (in a patronizing voice):

'You know, if I was you, I would ...'
'You really should ...'

These manipulative suggestions do not give the individual the respect and dignity to make their own choice.

Aggression is also evident in our vocal tone and speech pattern. We will now draw attention to vocal tones and speech patterns that are commonly associated with aggression. When being aggressive you probably would make use of the following.

A rigid, cold and sometimes patronizing vocal tone

A rigid vocal tone gives the impression of a firm unchangeable attitude of mind. This would give your listener a clear message that you are not willing to waver in your decision. While being aggressive, you would also sound cold, lacking in emotion, giving off the idea that you are distant and do not care much for their feelings. You would also employ a patronizing tone, speaking down to the other person in a belittling voice. A definite, cold, patronizing tone gives the message that what you are saying is true and that there is no room for discussion.

Harsh, loud voice

When being aggressive your vocal tone may usually be amplified; this serves to overwhelm or intimidate your listener. Harsh vocal volume aims to overpower the other to get your own way.

Fluent speech pattern with little hesitancy

The kind of fluency experienced when being aggressive is different from assertion, as it is without hesitation. It is a fast constant stream or barrage of your thoughts and opinions, without allowing the other person any room for feedback. It is often accusatory in over-emphasizing words that indicate blame. For example:

> 'And when *you* said that, well, I just could not believe *you* could be so *stupid.*'

We will now draw attention to the body language commonly associated with aggression. When being aggressive you probably would display the following.

Intense eye contact
Intense eye contact can be overwhelming and intimidating for the person with whom you are being aggressive. Remember, aggression encourages an overestimation of your worth. An arrogant 'staring out' or 'looking down' reinforces this unhealthy view of yourself. When being aggressive, then, your eye contact will be fixed and your gaze will not be inviting but piercing.

Taut facial expressions
When being aggressive your facial expressions would be hard and uninviting. For example, you may frown or scowl at the person if they voice a different view to yours. The muscles in your face would also look tense or firm. Aggression would also have you exaggerate your facial response in an attempt to down others' suggestions. For example, your eyes go heavenward and you raise your eyebrows in disbelief when your partner suggests going somewhere for an evening out. This facial expression serves to convey the message aggressively that you think your partner's suggestion defies all reasonableness. In turn she may think of herself as inferior so that she does not assert herself again.

Attacking and defensive body movement and posture
While being aggressive, your body movement may be attacking or closed and defensive. For example, you might wave your finger at the person or even in some instances shake your fist at them. Aggression can usually be identified in your body language through jerky, quick gestures. In addition, when not gesturing you may fold your arms tightly in an unapproachable, aloof fashion.

Your position when being aggressive would be attempting to intimidate the other. For instance, you may sit with your arms behind your head, which is a superior pose. Aggressively pacing when discussing an issue gives off the message that you are running out of patience. Setting your position physically higher than the other person or talking so close that it invades their space is also a hallmark of aggressive intimidation.

Above we have discussed speech, vocal tones and body language that would indicate that you were being aggressive. We will now highlight how you can identify when you are being passive.

Identifying passivity

As we have stated, passivity is all about avoiding the discomfort of conflict and attempting to please others, even at your own expense. We will now highlight the particular statements that are commonly associated with passivity. This list can be used as an indicator for you to see whether you are being assertive or passive. When being passive your behaviour would include:

Rambling, hesitant, approval-seeking 'I' statements

Passivity can be identified by 'I' statements that are long-winded, difficult to catch and easily misunderstood. For instance:

'I wondered whether . . . er . . . I . . . could . . . em . . . well, you know . . .'

When you employ rambling and hesitant 'I' statements they are not succinct. This means your point is easily missed or dismissed. Within these rambling and hesitant 'I' statements are also approval-seeking statements that undermine the possibility of others listening or acting on your preferences. For example, sandwiched in the rambling and hesitant 'I' statements may be excuses for what you are about to say, such as:

'As you are here, can I just mention . . .'
'I would not usually mention this, but . . .'
'I am sorry to have to mention . . .'

This justifying is aimed at softening what you are about to say. This is so that the other person does not see you as such a threat and potentially disapprove of you. In addition to the rambling 'I' statements and the excuses, there is also apologetic permission-seeking. Apologetic permission-seeking is also a sign of passivity as it again is approval-seeking. For example, once stating your preference in a rambled, excusing way you may also add at the end:

'I am sorry I had to bother you with this . . .'
'I really hope I have not put you out with what I have said . . .'

This apologizing weakens the impact of what you are attempting to assert. By apologizing and seeking the other person's permission, you have handed over full control to them. The reason for this is that apologetic permission-seeking conveys the message that their feelings and opinions are far more important than your own.

In summary, be aware of rambling and hesitant 'I' statements which start with excusing yourself and end with apologetic permission-seeking, as they are an indication of passivity.

Putting down your preferences or opinions
A downplaying of your preferences or opinions can further identify passivity. For example, while passively expressing your opinions you may notice that you have used the following:

'In my limited knowledge ...'
'I could be completely wrong but ...'

These statements go to dismiss your input into a situation or decision. In addition, you may put your entire self down when being passive. For instance:

'I really am useless ...'
'I can't seem to ever get anything right ...'

Entire self-downing can be used as a passive manipulation attempting to trigger off pity from others. Others' consoling words will go to reward your passivity and will also go to keep you stuck there.

Dismissing your own preferences and opinions
Passivity will have you valuing others' preferences, feelings and time above your own. For example, when enquiring or requesting something from others, you may say:

'I wonder perhaps whether you would mind ... but don't worry if you can't.'
'I really don't want to put you out, but ...'

These self-dismissive statements make it easy, almost inviting, for the other person to say 'no' to your request.

Rigid self-criticism
With rigid self-criticism, you become your own dictator. For example, you may say:

'I absolutely should not have ...'
'I am so sorry, I know I must ...'

These over-critical statements are passive as you are assuming all the

21

blame for a situation. Even if you did share a large portion of the responsibility by passively putting yourself down, you are elevating the other person into a superior position. Tacked on to the end of rigid self-critical statements are self-depreciation statements. For example, a self-depreciation statement may be:

'I am completely useless ...'
'I am totally stupid ...'

Rigid self-criticism and self-depreciation statements attempt to avoid confrontation by generating pity for you from the other person.

As with assertion and aggression, we will now draw attention to the particular vocal tones and speech patterns commonly associated with passivity. When being passive you would probably utilize the following.

A soft, quiet vocal tone
A soft, quiet vocal tone is an indication of a lack of confidence about what you are saying. Passivity can be identified in being over-warm in your speech. The tone may even be monotonous, without the natural use of modulation.

Vocal volume that tapers off
When being passive your vocal tone may start loud enough but will most probably taper off. This will undermine your message as it becomes increasingly difficult for the other person to hear what you are trying to say. This will result in them easily missing or dismissing your preference or opinion.

Uncertain speech pattern with a changeable pace
A speech pattern that highlights passivity is stifled and uncertain. It would contain many 'er' and 'um' sentence fillers, and would perhaps have long pauses. The pace of your speech would also change, perhaps becoming faster as you approach the main point you are trying to assert. Your uncertain speech pattern with a changeable pace conveys the message of a lack of inner conviction and certainty in what you are saying.

To conclude this section we will draw attention to the body language commonly associated with passivity. When being passive you would probably display the following.

Evasive eye contact
When being passive you would rarely look the other person in the eye. More often you will be looking down or away. This gives a clear message of shame or a lack of confidence.

Uncomfortable facial expressions

While being passive, your facial expressions will look and feel uncomfortable. They will also be incongruent with the message you are conveying. For instance, you may smile inappropriately when giving serious feedback to someone.

Tense distracting body movements

Passivity can be identified by tense distracting body movements which signal nervousness. For example, your shoulders may be hunched and your arms crossed while stating your preference. You may also be rather twitchy, shuffling around on the spot throughout the interaction. In some cases, you may even obscure your mouth with your hand while stating your preference. All these tense body movements aim to create a safe, protective distance between you and those with whom you are attempting to assert yourself. They work against you, though, detracting from your message and letting your listener know how nervous you are.

The above list is not exhaustive. You may well be able to add to it from your own experience. However, it serves as a basic framework for you to be able to identify whether you are being assertive, aggressive or passive. We will now focus on aiding you to identify what general beliefs underpin each of these three modes of communication.

Identifying beliefs underpinning assertion, aggression and passivity in the context of an ABC framework

Beliefs are our personal evaluations that we make and hold about ourselves, others and the world. For your assertion coaching to be truly successful, you will need to learn how to discriminate between healthy and unhealthy beliefs. Healthy beliefs fuel healthy behaviour such as assertion, and unhealthy beliefs will fuel unhealthy behaviour such as aggression or passivity. These evaluations or beliefs have a profound influence on our emotions and behaviours. This is the main tenet of the therapeutic approach we employ in this book. This therapeutic approach is called Rational Emotive Behaviour Therapy (REBT) and was pioneered by the famous American psychologist Dr Albert Ellis in the mid 1950s. REBT breaks down people's emotional and behavioural problems into an ABC framework.

The ABC framework provides an accessible, easy-to-use system that will help you identify the specific beliefs that are driving your unhealthy emotions and behaviours. The theory behind this model states that our emotions and behaviours (C – emotional and behavioural Consequences) are not directly created by what happens to us at point A (Activating Event); rather our Beliefs (B) mainly fuel them.

Understanding how to use the ABCs to guide you through your emotional and behavioural problems is much like learning to read a map. Rather than always having to ask for directions to every destination that's new for you, it saves you time and energy to master how to read a map effectively for yourself so that you can find your own way. REBT encourages you to become proficient at self-therapy using the map of the ABC framework to guide you through your problems. This saves you time and resources, as you don't have to consult a therapist for directions every time you are having emotional or behavioural difficulties. In effect, you use the map of the ABCs to aid you in becoming efficient at using the REBT skills to guide you through and overcome your particular problem at that time. We will now briefly explain how you can use the ABC format to identify specific unhealthy beliefs that are fuelling either your aggression or your passivity.

Understanding the ABCs

As previously stated, the A in the ABC framework stands for an activating event, a trigger for the beliefs we hold about ourselves, others or the world. In effect, the trigger is much like a doctor's patella hammer which hits just the right spot to spark a reaction in us. This activating event at A triggers our beliefs at B. These beliefs at B can be unhealthy or healthy. If the beliefs are unhealthy they will fuel an unhealthy emotional and behavioural consequence, and conversely if the beliefs are healthy they will fuel a healthy emotion and behaviour as a consequence. We will explain this further by using John and Colin's example, so please do not despair if on first reading it seems a little difficult to grasp.

When teaching our clients how to use the ABCs in understanding and overcoming their own disturbance, we first point out that they will initially start understanding the process after they have experienced the C (consequences), then usually it is on reflection that they identify the A (activating event) that triggered their Bs (beliefs). We help our clients to remember this sequence by using the acronym CAB. As a taxicab transports you to your desired destination, using the letters CAB gives you the order you can intervene at assessing your problem. For example, if you feel an unhealthy negative emotion and act unhealthily, whether aggressively or passively, in a situation – there is your C. You then need to identify the activating event. To do this you may ask yourself, 'If there was one thing that I could have taken away from that situation that would have prevented me from experiencing my unhealthy negative emotion or behaviour, what would that have been?' This usually gives you the insight into the theme of your specific unhealthy belief (please refer to John or Colin's example to understand how this works in practice). Once you have identified the A, you can then move on to identify your unhealthy B, and then construct a healthy B, which will fuel a new effect (E) in your emotion and behaviour.

In summary, if you wish to travel from A to E, catch a CAB. Simple? Yes. But it is not easy. For this reason we will highlight how to employ the ABC framework by using John and Colin's example. Although we will mainly refer to John's example initially, exactly the same steps are used in assessing passivity. To avoid being overly repetitious, after John's example we will highlight the beliefs that Colin identified using the steps we are about to teach you, rather than stating the steps in detail again.

Using the ABC framework with beliefs that underpin aggression

As you may recall, John had an anger problem, which was triggered mainly when he had disagreements with his partner. We shall use his example to explain the ABC assessment process.

Step 1: Ensure that your main problem is unhealthy anger
The first step in using the ABC framework is to identify your C. It is important that when doing this you are sure that the emotion you are assessing is indeed unhealthy anger (if in any doubt refer to Windy Dryden's book *10 Steps to Positive Living* (Sheldon Press, 1994), using Step 6 as a guide). John was sure that his main unhealthy emotion was unhealthy anger as his behaviour highlighted this. This gave him a specific emotional consequence to work on. (John also experienced anxiety and guilt, but as a matter of course we only assess and work through one emotion at a time, otherwise the ABC process can become extremely confusing.)

Step 2: Select a concrete example of your unhealthy anger
The second step in using the ABC framework is to identify your A. When doing this it is important to be as specific as possible; for this reason a concrete example is preferable. The reason for using a real – and, if possible, recent – example is that it will give you greater insight into the specific beliefs you were holding at that time. John decided to use a recent argument where he ended up punching the living room door and kicking the wall.

Step 3: Describe the situation
The third step is to describe the situation you were in at the time you experienced the unhealthy negative emotion. John described how he and his partner were arguing about a decision he had made which she refused to accept.

Step 4: Identify the A (the critical aspect of the situation you were most disturbed about)

This is the stage where you can grasp the critical point that triggered the unhealthy beliefs leading to your unhealthy consequence at C. To do this, ask yourself, 'If there was one thing that I could have taken away from that situation that would have prevented me from experiencing my unhealthy negative emotion or behaviour, what would that have been?' John found it helpful to peruse some general categories that are associated with unhealthy anger being triggered. We have separated these into two categories: first, 'unhealthy discomfort anger', which is to do with discomfort to one's environment or personal domain; second, 'unhealthy ego anger', which is when one perceives that one's personality or self-worth is threatened. We have briefly cited these two lists below:

Unhealthy discomfort anger

- Frustration.
- Injustice.
- Insult.
- Threat.
- Transgression against a rule.
- Socially offensive behaviour.

Unhealthy ego anger

- Insufficient respect or deference.
- Rejection.
- Being criticized.
- Being ridiculed.
- Being blamed.
- Anger at self-violation of non-moral personal rule or standard (act of commission or omission).

John identified the critical point of his activating event as insufficient respect from his partner. At this point we did not dispute whether that assumption was true or not. We encourage you to do the same. To get to the unhealthy belief underpinning your aggression, it is important not to check whether the activating event is true: just assume for now that it is. Once you have identified your unhealthy belief then you can challenge the authenticity of your assumption at A.

Step 5: Identifying the unhealthy belief that fuelled your aggression

So far, we have identified the A and the C in the ABC model. For John his sequence at this point looked like this:

Situation = Partner not accepting a decision I had made.

A = She thinks she is right and I am wrong.
B = ?
C = Emotional: unhealthy anger.
Behavioural: punching door and kicking wall.

John was now ready to identify his unhealthy beliefs that were fuelling his disturbance. It is at this point in the ABC framework that John identified the four beliefs that are characteristic of unhealthy thinking and consequently unhealthy anger. It is important for you, if you are to use the ABC framework efficiently, to have a general grasp of what REBT has identified and specified as beliefs that are characteristic of unhealthy thinking. Let us explain these four belief types in the context of John's specific example. Here are John's specific unhealthy beliefs at B:

- *Rigid demanding beliefs*
  The general beliefs that fuel aggression are initially rigid and demanding. These beliefs do not allow for flexibility in any way. They are extreme and fixed and are not reality-based. For example, when being aggressive, John identified the fact that he rigidly believed:

  'I must prove I am right, and she is wrong.'

These rigid demanding beliefs left him vulnerable to aggression as they went beyond any realistic expectation.

- *Awfulizing beliefs*
  Awfulizing beliefs are associated with aggression as they overestimate the badness of an event, changing it into a horror. For example, while being aggressive, John believed:

  'If she does not accept that she is wrong and I am right it will be absolutely horrible.'

John's awfulizing beliefs got him to exaggerate the badness of the moment, transforming his unmet preferences to a real end-of-the-world horror.

- *Low frustration tolerance (LFT) beliefs*
  Low frustration tolerance beliefs encourage you to underestimate vastly your emotional stamina to handle disappointment. Fuelling John's aggression were LFT beliefs such as:

  'It's intolerable that she thinks she is right and I am wrong.'

LFT beliefs are just not true. John could tolerate disappointment and certainly did not die from it. Believing these low frustration tolerance beliefs will keep you aggressive, because you would do anything to stop the event from happening.

- *Self-elevation and depreciation of others*
  Aggression encourages you to put others down and to elevate yourself. For example, while John was being aggressive with his girlfriend he would put her down in his mind by believing:

  'Damn her for not seeing it my way.'

This self-elevation and depreciation of others fuelled his aggression as it maintained a superior view of his opinions and preferences.

Using the above, John's final ABC assessment looked something like this:

Situation = Partner not accepting a decision I had made.
A = She thinks she is right and I am wrong.
B = 'I must prove I am right, and she is wrong.'
 'If she does not accept that she is wrong and I am right it will be absolutely horrible.'
 'It's intolerable that she thinks she is right and I am wrong.'
 'Damn her for not seeing it my way.'
C = Emotional: unhealthy anger.
 Behavioural: punching door and kicking wall.

John was now ready to challenge his unhealthy anger-creating beliefs. We will go on to show you how you can do this in Chapter 3. Colin also followed exactly the same step-by-step process using the ABC framework to assess his unhealthy beliefs that fuelled his passivity. We will highlight what these were, bearing in mind that Colin followed the above steps to assess his ABC accurately.

Using the ABC framework with beliefs that underpin passivity

Colin used a specific situation at work where he was avoiding confronting a business colleague. We will pick up his ABC assessment at Step 4.

Step 4: Identifying the unhealthy belief that fuelled your passivity
Colin's sequence at this point looked like this:

Situation = Will need to confront colleague in business meeting.
A = Hurting my colleague's feelings.
B = ?

C = Emotional: anxiety.
Behavioural: passivity and avoidance of subject.

Using REBT's identified unhealthy beliefs, Colin assessed his specific unhealthy beliefs at B to be the following:

- *Rigid demanding beliefs*
  Colin believed:

  'I must not hurt my colleague's feelings.'

Colin explained that he lived his life by this rigid rule that was impossible to fulfil. Consequently, he was stuck in a passive way of communicating: he dared not assert himself because when you are assertive others can feel hurt about what you say.

- *Awfulizing beliefs*
  As with aggression, Colin's passivity was also fuelled by awfulizing beliefs, such as:

  'If I hurt my colleague's feelings, it is terrible.'

Colin held these awfulizing beliefs which led him to over-value the badness of the possible consequence of his assertion. He firmly believed there could be nothing worse than someone hurting over something he said. This overestimation of how bad things could be made him stay passive.

- *Low frustration tolerance (LFT) beliefs*
  Colin falsely believed that he did not have the resources to cope with the possible eventualities of his assertion. Colin identified the following LFT belief:

  'I could not stand it if I hurt my colleague's feelings.'

LFT beliefs assume that the results of your assertion will go beyond your coping level. These beliefs lead you to assume illogically that you will not be able to endure or withstand the discomfort of assertion. Consequently, you will convince yourself to remain quiet.

- *Self-depreciation and other-elevation*
  Passivity relies on self-depreciation and elevation of the other. This means that you devalue yourself while you fulfil the conditions of your rigid beliefs. Colin identified his self-depreciation belief to be:

  'If I don't hurt my colleague I am a good person; if my colleague feels hurt at what I say or do then I am totally worthless.'

This conditional self-acceptance belief fuelled passivity, as Colin was less likely to take any risk of triggering hurt or disapproval in another by asserting himself. Others sensed this through experience, and hence made unreasonable requests because they knew they could get away with it.

Using the above, Colin's final ABC assessment looked something like this:

> Situation = Will need to confront colleague in business meeting.
> A = Hurting my colleague's feelings.
> B = 'I must not hurt my colleague's feelings.'
> 'If I hurt my colleague's feelings, it is terrible.'
> 'I could not stand it if I hurt my colleague's feelings.'
> 'If I don't hurt my colleague I am a good person; if my colleague feels hurt at what I say or do then I am totally worthless.'
> C = Emotional: anxiety.
> Behavioural: passivity and avoidance of subject.

Colin was now ready to challenge his unhealthy beliefs that led to passivity. Before he or John did so, however, they also set up a healthy alternative belief to take the unhealthy belief's place. It is important to replace the beliefs that fuel aggression and passivity with healthy, more rational ones, as this will fuel your assertive behaviour. This means that although you may not be able to change your activating event, you can change your response to it by holding a healthy belief. So, for example, your boss may continue to shout at you, which is your specific A and is somewhat out of your control. What you can change are your beliefs in regard to her shouting. This hopefully will fuel a healthy C. We will now highlight the beliefs that REBT purports lead to healthy negative emotions and consequently healthy assertion.

General beliefs underpinning assertion
Preferential beliefs
The general beliefs that underpin assertion are initially preferential. Preferential beliefs are flexible in their expectation and appraisal of reality. For example, when asserting yourself you may flexibly believe:

> 'I would like to get my preference met, but there is no law that decrees that I must do so . . .'
> 'I wish to have this person's approval, but I do not need it . . .'

These preferential beliefs are flexible and keep you focused on a more realistic outcome.

Non-awfulizing beliefs
Assertion is also fuelled by non-awfulizing beliefs. These non-awfulizing beliefs are an accurate evaluation of the badness of a negative event. For example, while asserting yourself you may believe:

'If my preference is not met this time it is unfortunate, but not the end of the world for me.'

These non-awfulizing beliefs aid you in not exaggerating the badness of the moment, or the badness of the possible consequences of your assertion.

High frustration tolerance (HFT) beliefs

High frustration tolerance beliefs also fuel assertion. These beliefs realistically appraise your tolerance levels in the face of negative events, i.e. what you can and cannot cope with. When being assertive you may healthily believe:

'Although it is uncomfortable not having my preference met, I can stand it,'
or
'I can stand the disapproval of this person, it will not kill me.'

HFT beliefs rightly assume that the results of your assertion will most probably not cause you unbearable pain, resulting in your disintegrating on the spot. They realistically assume that you can stand most eventualities, even though you may face a struggle.

Self-, other- and life-acceptance

It can be said that assertion rests on the philosophy of self-, other- and life-acceptance. For example, while asserting yourself your acceptance beliefs may be:

'I fully accept myself as a fallible human being who will make mistakes.'
'I fully accept that others are just as deserving as I am.'
'I fully accept that my way is not the only way.'

These self-, other- and life-acceptance beliefs fuel assertion as they are accurate in appraising your worth in consideration of others.

As you have most probably observed, healthy beliefs underpin healthy assertion and unhealthy beliefs will maintain unhealthy behaviour such as aggression or passivity. If from the above list you have identified unhealthy beliefs characteristic of aggression or passivity, do not be disheartened. No one is a complete slave to their unhealthy beliefs or behaviour, even if these traits have been present for many years. What you have learned you can unlearn, and what you have taught yourself you can unteach yourself! So although you may have identified some unhealthy beliefs, that does not mean you are doomed. In Chapter 2 we will show you that you can, through persistent focused effort, make positive changes and become assertive.

Summary

In this chapter we have defined what assertion is and what it is not. We have shown you how to distinguish between assertion, aggression and passivity. We have identified the healthy and unhealthy beliefs that underpin these three modes of communicating. Yet this will not be enough to get you started. In the next chapter, we will highlight some thinking blocks to assertion, and teach you how to coach yourself over them.

2

Dealing with your fears of assertion

Let us start by illustrating how your fears can stop you from being assertive. When approaching a red traffic light while driving your car, what do you do? Well, obviously you stop your vehicle. You most probably found that after some practice this manoeuvre is almost automatic. Do you regularly recite the Highway Code, consciously stating the reasons for stopping? No, you just automatically apply the brakes, and stop. Your fears have a similar effect on your assertion. You do not think through why you do not assert yourself, you just automatically apply the brakes and stop yourself.

In this chapter, we will help you identify and overcome the unhealthy beliefs that underpin those fears that have been stopping you from healthy assertion. Before showing you how to challenge these beliefs, we will discuss eight principles of self-care and respect for others. These principles stress realistic equality for all people. The principles will, we hope, act as a good motivational pull for you to challenge your unhealthy beliefs, and be assertive even when it seems very difficult.

Good coaching relies on the principles of self-care and respect for others

Assertion is motivated by the principles of self-care and respect for others. Before specifying the principles, let us define what we mean by self-care and respect for others.

Self-care essentially means considering your self-interest first. Self-care is literally giving serious attention and thought to your own preferences or interests. Active self-care means that you are seriously concerned with your own life, and prioritizing time to develop your own talents to their full potential. Self-care encourages you not to forsake your own development temporarily unless there is very good reason to do so. The principle of self-care on its own is not healthy; in fact, too much self-care can lead to selfishness. With this in mind, the principle of self-care needs to be tempered with respect for others.

Respect for others encourages you to acknowledge that we live in a community with many individuals who have their own set of goals, standards and preferences. Respect for others aids you in showing appropriate consideration for others, not as superior or inferior, but as equal to you. Respect for others literally means considering another individual in relation to yourself. This principle keeps us flexible when our preferences are temporarily not met, and so leads to healthy compromise when necessary.

We will now state some of the principles that underpin self-care and respect for others. As you will notice, none of these principles advocates the irrational idea that any individual is worthier than any other in having their preferences met. The following principles provide a framework on which healthy interaction and relationships can be based. The principles of self-care and respect for others build positive connections between you and others, allowing for personal expression and assertion of opinions throughout difficult interactions. These principles are very important for your assertion coaching to be a success. In our practice as therapists, we have observed that when an individual is not asserting herself or himself then one or more of the following principles is being negated.

Principle 1

Self-care encourages you to say 'no' when you deem it appropriate to do so. Respect for others encourages you to accept that this principle also applies to all other people

How many times have you said 'yes' when really you wanted to say 'no'? With appropriate self-care, you assert your preference without guilt. With self-care, you accept that you do not have to come up with a reasonable or convincing explanation for declining the request of another. If you do not *want* to do it, you do not *have* to do it! If this seems a little harsh, look at the alternative: those with *low* self-care and *too much* respect for others. For example, Joan falsely believed that she just 'could not say no', especially to her husband. By not saying 'no', Joan avoided any temporary discomfort, but the amount of time it cost her in energy and resources was incredible. Joan learned that the temporary comfort gained by avoiding saying 'no' did not usually outweigh the future inconvenience that she experienced.

In addition, how often do individuals who 'can't say no' get time to meet their own needs? Not a lot. Their time is taken up with pleasing others. Consequently, a loss of identity ensues where they no longer know what they want or enjoy, losing confidence in themselves, and a low sense of self-worth is usually the result. The long-term disadvantages surely outweigh the short-term comfort of avoiding saying 'no'.

To conclude Principle 1, accepting that you and others can say 'no' saves you time and energy by reducing your engagement in personally unproductive tasks. Exercising your self-care in respect to saying 'no' when you deem it appropriate without the need for explanation also adds to your confidence in your new assertion coaching.

Principle 2

Self-care encourages you to express your emotions, opinions and beliefs when you deem it appropriate to do so. Respect for others encourages you to accept that this principle also applies to all other people

You are a unique individual. There is no one else like you in the world. Even if you are an identical twin, you and your twin would each have different life experiences, hence making you unique individuals. Accepting your individuality means that you also accept that your emotions, opinions and beliefs will be as individual as you are. To deny this principle is to show too much respect for others and to negate your self-care. Assertion encourages an open, honest expression of yourself when you deem it appropriate. It logically follows that you will have distinct emotions, opinions and beliefs from those of others. As this will inevitably be the case it is not unreasonable or rude to express these differences. To deny your emotions, opinions and beliefs is to deny your individuality. Suppress this long enough and you will lose sight of your self-identity.

Take, for example, wig-wearing Jonas Hanway. He lived in London during the 1750s when, if it rained, it was customary and acceptable only for women to use umbrellas. Yet Jonas, wanting to preserve his appearance, expressed his preference in using an umbrella. For over thirty years he suffered derision and criticism, many claiming that he was an 'insult to manhood'. Yet every time it rains are we not glad that Jonas stuck to his guns and exercised enough self-care to express his individual wish? Take the risk of being different: those that fear change will laugh, but do not negate your self-care on account of the negative thinking of others.

Respect for others also aids you in accepting that others will have their own idiosyncratic emotions, opinions and beliefs. They do not have to agree with you and you do not have to agree with them. They have the right to their opinions, although you may believe them to be wrong.

In summary, Principle 2 encourages you to express your emotions, opinions and beliefs when you deem it appropriate. This leads to maintaining your individuality, and it increases your self-confidence. Celebrate your individuality, do not deny it. Applying Principle 2 also encourages a realistic acceptance that others will not always agree with you or see it your way. Accepting others' expressions of individuality will lead to communication that is more constructive. This in turn will encourage you to remain assertive, even in difficult situations.

Principle 3

Self-care encourages you to acknowledge that you will make mistakes and accept yourself for making them. Respect for others encourages you to accept that this principle also applies to all other people

Self-care encourages you to accept the reality of your fallibility. Being human intrinsically means that you will make mistakes. Assertion coaching strongly relies on this principle because accepting your fallibility will encourage you to take responsibility for your mistakes, and then face the consequences in a healthy manner. This principle leads to greater self-care, as acknowledging and accepting your fallibility limits your experiencing self-defeating emotions such as guilt and shame after making a mistake. Accepting your fallible nature keeps you assertive and reduces the risk of your allowing others to control you. This was John's experience. He would feel guilt and shame after communicating aggressively, and then attempted to atone for his mistake by engaging in 'right' behaviours to correct or neutralize the wrong. He would be over-helpful, engaging in more household chores, and also promising to get 'help'. His girlfriend would then capitalize on his guilt, delighting in getting him to do arduous tasks as a penalty. After a short time he would become annoyed at this, and the aggressive–overhelpful cycle would start over again.

By accepting your tendency to make mistakes, you are no longer vulnerable to engaging in correct or neutralizing behaviour as penance for your mistake. This principle leads you to maintain appropriate self-care, for you do not irrationally think that others are more worthy or deserving of your time because you acted badly to them. It also aids in maintaining your assertion skills even if you think you have acted particularly badly.

To conclude Principle 3, accepting your fallibility will dispel the notion that others are worthier than you are because they have not made a mistake at a time when you did. This principle leads to greater self-care as you maintain a realistic healthy view of yourself, and as a consequence assert yourself appropriately when others try to control you. Respect for others in this regard encourages you to accept others' fallible nature, as well as your own.

Principle 4

Self-care encourages you to be yourself without believing you have to be different for another person's benefit. Respect for others encourages you to accept that this principle also applies to all other people

Self-care encourages you to be true to yourself and not change for another person's benefit. Since as humans we are complex, we have different sides to ourselves. We can be easy-going or strict, friendly or unfriendly, tough or tender. When we demand that we have to be perceived a certain way, we may go against being true to ourselves for fear of being viewed as different. For example, Colin always wished to be perceived as an 'easy-going, decent' individual. Liz, his partner, suggested that he stay in his car when picking up his son from his ex-partner's home. This was something Colin did not wish to do. He was now faced with a dilemma: would he be true to himself and assert his preference, or conform because he 'must' be perceived as an 'easy-going, decent' individual at all times?

Adopting Principle 4 encouraged Colin to accept that he was complex, and so would not be consistently 'easy-going and decent' with everything and everyone, all the time. This is just one example. Principle 4 can be applied to various self-care issues, for instance not being falsely cheerful when you actually feel miserable. Applying Principle 4 is good for assertion coaching as it inhibits you from acting in a false way. This means that you would not put on a mask for the benefit of others, but act in a way which is a true representation of how you really think or feel.

Respect for others encourages you to accept that other people also do not have to put on a mask just for your benefit. This leads to greater flexibility in your interaction with others, allowing them to be themselves and not expecting them to have to perform just to please you.

In summary, Principle 4 is a healthy, more reality-based view of our complexity. It allows you to be miserable and cheerful, and not to have to adapt or be false just to please others. Showing respect for others in this regard means that you do not demand others are always a certain way just to please you.

Principle 5

Self-care allows you to be able to change your mind, even if this inconveniences others. Respect for others encourages you to accept that this principle also applies to all other people

We live in a world of change where there are probably no absolute guarantees. Healthy self-care relies on this realistic theory as it allows you to assert your change of mind, even if it is a nuisance to others. Through the passage of time and the environment we live in, our interests and choices are likely to shift. This is realistic and, most of all, normal for healthy adaptive individuals. The alternative to Principle 5 is sticking by a decision out of fear of inconveniencing others.

This was one of Denise's obstacles. She hit the brakes on her assertion because she believed that if you change your mind, which you absolutely should not do, then something is wrong with you. As already pointed out in other principles of self-care, agreeing with this unrealistic idea leads to great discomfort and frustration for you in the long run. Denise's fear of changing her mind meant, for instance, that she could never allow herself to return new purchases, such as clothes, to the shops from which she had bought them.

Respect for others encourages you to accept that others will at times change their mind. This may inconvenience you, but it will give you opportunity to practise high frustration tolerance for a while. It may help to bear in mind at those times that life could well be spelt H.A.S.S.L.E.

In summary, it is more realistic and helpful for you to acknowledge that you will at times change your mind. This will most probably inconvenience others, even if your change of mind is improving something that is inadequate. Respect for others also encourages remembering that others will inconvenience you when they change their mind – which will happen. This principle is best summed up by Aldous Huxley, who wrote, 'Consistency is contrary to nature, contrary to life. The only completely consistent people are the dead.'

A word of caution. Following this principle doesn't mean that you can break your commitment to a person just because something or someone more exciting has come along. Living according to Principle 5 is difficult! It involves respecting the commitments that you make to others accepting that important changes occur in your life. It does not involve letting others down for trivial reasons.

Principle 6

Self-care allows you to make decisions that others find illogical without necessarily having to give an explanation. Respect for others encourages you to accept that this principle also applies to all other people

As with the principles stated previously, Principle 6 fosters self-care resulting in healthy assertion. It does this because it advocates that you are the ultimate judge of what you believe and what you do. Consequently, if someone believes that your decision is illogical, that is no reason why you have to explain or change your decision. If you do negate this principle and give an explanation when one is not warranted, or change because of them, you are relinquishing your right to make up your own mind. Therefore, you are effectively handing over control of your life to the other person. Self-care in this respect keeps you as ultimate judge of your thoughts, emotions and behaviour, enabling you to accept full responsibility for them.

With regard to Principle 6, respect for others encourages you not to become judge and jury of others. For instance, Joan's husband would demand explanations from her for decisions he did not agree with. If he had applied Principle 6 then he would have accepted that Joan did not have to answer to him as if he were some great authority or higher wisdom. He would have stopped assuming responsibility for Joan's decisions which would have saved him time and energy in tirelessly trying to correct what he viewed as illogical decisions.

Applying Principle 6 means that you accept that other individuals have the ultimate authority to be their own judge. This fosters mutual respect and maintains healthy boundaries, aiding in a more fulfilling relationship for both you and the other person.

To summarize, Principle 6 leads to good assertion coaching, as your assertion is not dependent on others reassuring you that your view is logical. You may seek appropriate feedback before making a decision, but ultimately make the decision yourself. By doing this you exercise self-care, accepting that not everyone will agree with your decision. This keeps you as the ultimate judge of your thoughts, emotions and behaviour. Respect for others also helps you to accept that others are not answerable to you in the decisions they make. As Joan's husband learned, you do not have to agree with someone for it to be a good decision.

Principle 7

Self-care encourages you to decline the responsibility of finding solutions to others' problems. Respect for others encourages you to accept that this principle also applies to all other people

We are all ultimately responsible for our own physical, psychological and emotional well-being. We may regularly wish others well and genuinely desire that good things happen to them. Yet they are ultimately responsible for their life and their problems, as we are for ours. It is true that we can trigger off feelings of comfort or pleasure when we do what they want, but this is only temporary. We are not in a position or do not have the power to solve their problems or correct them – that authority ultimately is theirs. This principle leads to greater self-care as it realistically helps you accept your limitations. For example, George learned to apply this principle with his family. Following this he found that he no longer exhausted himself attempting to rescue them from themselves. Understanding this principle also explained to George why he had repeatedly tried hard to aid his sister, but she always seemed to persist in making the same stupid mistakes.

Respect for others in relation to this principle encourages you not to rely solely on others for solutions to your problems. This is your responsibility, and one of the main reasons why we are all blessed with our own thinking ability. It is our personal responsibility to solve, overcome or manage our own problems. Respect for others encourages you to accept that others, even significant others, have the right to say 'This is not my problem, you sort it out.'

In summary, Principle 7 leads to greater self-care as it allows you to decline responsibility for finding solutions to others' problems. You can do this because we are all ultimately responsible for our own lives. Respect for others encourages you to accept that others can decline the responsibility for solving your issues. Applying Principle 7 leads to you to learn to be reliant on yourself for solutions, and this makes you more adept at solving future problems. However, applying Principle 7 does not preclude you from offering other people solutions to their problems. It means that you give them the responsibility for whether or not they act on your advice.

Principle 8

Self-care encourages you to state your ignorance of, or lack of interest in, a matter without feeling ashamed or embarrassed about doing so. Respect for others encourages you to accept that this principle also applies to all other people

It is important to be able to declare your ignorance in a matter without feeling ashamed. Socrates stated that he 'knew nothing except the fact of his ignorance'. Socrates was observing a common human experience, which is that the more we come to know, the less we realize we knew. That is why an expert can be defined as someone who comes to know more and more about less and less. Consequently it is logical to conclude that there will be times when we do not understand, or are ignorant about, something that another person seems to know a lot about. That is no reason to feel ashamed, for what human knows everything? Subsequently one explanation may not be enough and we may need to hear it a number of times to understand the matter fully. For life to be a learning experience we are required to admit to not understanding a matter, and will at times need something explained several times again. This is all part of good self-care.

Principle 8 also advocates asserting your lack of interest in something without shame or embarrassment. This is also good self-care as no one else has the right to judge what you will like and what you will not like. It is not realistic to believe that you will be interested in everything the world or others have to offer. Assertion encourages open expression of your likes and dislikes. Therefore you will at times assert your lack of interest in certain matters that you find boring or of no appeal to you. The alternative to applying this principle is that you will have occasions where you engage in tedious activities. This will take time away from your own vitally absorbing interests.

Principle 8 leads to respect for others as it encourages an acceptance of others when they voice their ignorance or lack of interest in a matter that you find riveting. They have the right to express a lack of interest on any matter. This fosters respect for others, as you accept others non-judgementally when they assert their ignorance or indifference.

In summary, Principle 8 promotes asserting your ignorance or lack of interest in a matter. This is healthy as it is a realistic appraisal of your knowledge and adds to your further learning. In addition, Principle 8 takes into account the many individual interests that exist. This principle encourages you to be honest with others. It also encourages respect for others when they do not understand something we know, or are indifferent about something we are interested in.

So, to recap, here are the eight principles underpinning self-care and respect for others:

1 Say 'no' when you deem it appropriate, and accept that others may do so too.
2 Express your emotions, opinions and beliefs when you deem it appropriate, and accept that others may do so too.
3 Acknowledge that you will make mistakes, and accept yourself for making them. This applies to others too.
4 Be yourself without believing you have to be different for someone else's benefit. Accept that others can be themselves too.
5 Allow yourself to change your mind even if this inconveniences others, and accept that others may do so too.
6 Accept that you can make decisions others find illogical but do not necessarily have to give an explanation. This applies to others too.
7 Decline the responsibility of finding solutions to others' problems, and accept that this applies to others too.
8 Feel comfortable about stating your ignorance or lack of interest, and accept that this applies to others too.

After considering these eight principles, you are ready to focus on the unhealthy belief that may be underpinning your fear of assertion. To be able to overcome your fear of assertion you need to admit ownership of these beliefs, rather than blaming others or unfortunate life events for not asserting yourself. To do so will require you to take emotional responsibility.

Coaching starts with emotional responsibility

To be successfully assertive you will need to accept that your thinking, your emotions and your behaviour belong to you. You largely determine how you respond to people through the view you hold about the situation you are in. It is a basic tenet of Rational Emotive Behaviour Therapy (REBT) that no one can 'make' you feel anything: you are responsible for your own thoughts and emotions. This is liberating as it means nobody has complete control over you, but you can decide whether to respond in a healthy or unhealthy way to most situations. Emotional responsibility also encourages you to accept that you cannot influence others' thoughts, emotions and behaviour directly.

If someone decides to feel hurt because of your assertion, then that belongs to him or her, not you. Of course, emotional responsibility does not advocate a belligerent, insensitive approach to how you treat others. It is not to be used to justify or excuse cruel, tactless and malicious behaviour. That would be a misapplication of this principle. What emotional responsibility does encourage is individual accountability; this prevents the blaming of others for aspects of your life that you can take action to change. (For a full discussion on emotional responsibility, see Step 1 in Windy Dryden's *10 Steps to Positive Living* (Sheldon Press, 1994).)

Once you accept emotional responsibility, you are ready to tackle your fears of assertion. We will now tackle each obstacle in turn, highlighting sound reasoning that will help you challenge your particular fear.

Overcome the fear of not being liked

Can you recall any human who has enjoyed universal acceptance? There has most probably not been one human being who has been liked by everyone all the time. Think of some of the individuals who stand out in history – Nelson Mandela, Eleanor Roosevelt, Martin Luther King, Emmeline Pankhurst, Mahatma Mohandas Gandhi, Jesus Christ. These individuals have been revered by many, yet there were those who did not like them. Some individuals even despised them enough to want to murder them. The reason for this is that there are billions of people with a variety of likes and dislikes. Attempting to please everyone is an impossible task – you will not be approved of all the time. Consequently, to demand that others 'must' like you all the time is going to fuel some very unhealthy behaviour. By rigidly thinking that you need others' approval you will hold back from being true to your own opinions, emotions and behaviour, and replace them with what you think others will view as acceptable.

Denise identified the fear of disapproval as a main obstacle to her becoming assertive. She overcame this fear of not being liked by holding a flexible belief about others' approval. After some discussion, she concluded:

> 'I wish others liked me, I may even work towards it, but I do not *need* their approval.'

Holding this flexible belief kept her acting assertively even if it threatened the way her friends or family viewed her. She also accepted the reality that not all people would like her opinions, beliefs and behaviour.

Overcome the fear of being rejected

Being rejected by someone is difficult to bear, especially when that individual may know you well. Yet if you hold the idea that rejection is beyond your tolerance level, you will view rejection as the end of the world, believing you have not got the ability to cope with it when it happens. This will fuel fear and anxiety about rejection, and as a result you will endeavour to avoid possible rejection at all costs. This avoidance can lead to passivity, as asserting yourself may seem far too risky because it could incur rejection from the person or group with whom you are being assertive. Passivity reinforces the idea that rejection really is the worst thing that could happen to you, and that you will not be able to bear it if it occurs. This creates a vicious cycle which, over time, will increase your unassertive behaviour.

To overcome this fear we encourage a more realistic appraisal of the badness of rejection, and your tolerance threshold in coping with it. Let us explain a realistic appraisal of rejection by calling upon Joan's experience. After some discussion Joan decided to hold the following healthy belief:

> 'Rejection is bad and I do not like it, but I am not immune from it happening. It isn't the end of the world, and although it's hard to handle, I can cope with it.'

This healthy appraisal led to more assertive behaviour, even when Joan believed rejection might have been a possible risk.

Actually, if rejection has been an issue for you for some time, we encourage you to put yourself in a position where you *are* rejected on a few occasions before asserting yourself. This may sound preposterous to you, but let us explain the rationale for doing this by means of an illustration. When you go to the doctor's for a flu jab, what is contained in the inoculation? It is a little of what you are attempting not to catch. The reason for this is that exposure to the feared virus creates antibodies in your blood. This gives you an immunity to what it is you are trying to avoid. The same principle applies for a psychological immunity to a feared event such as rejection. In order to build a higher resistance to feeling anxious about rejection, you need to expose yourself to it. If you think rationally about rejection, this exposure will give you a higher immunity and tolerance to rejection and inhibits you from disturbing yourself about it. Such exposure to rejection gives tangible evidence in your mind that rejection is bad but not catastrophic and, although uncomfortable, you can cope with it far better than you had previously expected. By holding the healthy belief and practising the suggested approach, the fear of rejection will no longer hinder you from being assertive.

Overcome the fear of being selfish

Many people hold back from assertion as they confuse assertive behaviour with being selfish. In an attempt to avoid selfishness they become selfless, putting others' interests first, and hence allowing others to dictate their lives for them. We make a keen distinction between selfishness and self-interest. We make this distinction between the two as self-interest leads to healthy assertion. Selfishness is defined as acting only in your own interest, with a disregard for others and their interests. When acting selfishly there is no give and take, it is all take. On the rare occasion you do give something, it is with great resentment or with only an immediate return in mind.

With self-interest you still act with your own benefit in mind but also with regard for others. It is based more on responding and initiating acts of self- and other-care. Self-interest allows for giving, as well as taking, in a relationship or friendship.

If this still seems too selfish for you then it would be appropriate to look at the alternative, a life of selflessness. This is where you negate your own interest in favour of pleasing others. In the long term, you will actually fail to get what you want from your relationships. The reason for this is that you are teaching the other person that your interests are of no concern, and that they are far more important as a human being than you are. Your spoiling others (which is what selflessness often amounts to) actually teaches them that your needs can be ignored. Therefore, you will be taken for granted and disrespected and will feel unloved – all the things you believed your selflessness would save you from.

To overcome this fear we encourage a healthy belief that gives you a realistic estimation of your worth. We promote a balanced view of your value. This is because an imbalance leads to unhealthy behaviour: too much self-worth (or what psychologists call narcissism) leads to selfishness, while not enough leads you to selflessness. To avoid the unhealthy consequences of this imbalance we suggest you hold the following healthy belief:

> 'I accept that I am of equal worth compared with all other people. I also accept that I have different strengths and weaknesses but these never make me inferior or superior to others.'

This healthy self-accepting belief will lead to behaviour that is assertive, as it promotes an active self-interest and prevents unhealthy selfishness or selflessness.

For example, after considering the concept of self-interest Denise realized that she too feared being perceived as selfish and so went to the other extreme of complete selflessness. This was particularly the case with her children. After taking on board this principle Denise decided to assert herself even if this was going to inconvenience her children. An opportunity arose when her son requested being picked up and driven home from his friend's house. This act was solely for her son's benefit, as she had 101 things to do at home, and to add to that sitting in traffic was not her favourite pastime. Denise agreed to his request but, acting in self-interest, she asserted to him on the way home that she wished him to reciprocate this act by cooking the supper that evening. While he was in the kitchen cooking, Denise relaxed in the lounge without feeling guilty. Denise had acted through self-interest for the first time. At the same time Denise was teaching her son the way of the world: that is, others' time and resources are to be respected through fair exchange.

Overcome the fear of hurting or upsetting others

This is a very common type of fear and one which can stop assertion dead in its tracks. This fear has kept people trapped in unhealthy relationships for years. It is how parents emotionally blackmail and manipulate their children, even when their children may be old enough to draw a pension.

Not challenging the fear of hurting another's feelings is precarious for your assertion coaching. The reason for this is that at the first sign of hurt in the other person you will feel guilty and subsequently stop your assertion. You will feel guilty because you erroneously believe that you directly caused that hurt. The best way to beat this fear and overcome the possible guilt is to reflect on the principle of emotional responsibility. You can do this by asking yourself whether it is logical to believe that you can make anyone do, or feel, anything. If you had that authority, you would be incredibly powerful and extremely rich. If you had the power to actually change people's emotions single-handedly, think of the good you could do. For example, just by saying a few words to a depressed individual you could transform them and 'make' them happy.

In reality though, you do not possess the power to make an individual feel happy or depressed. To reinforce this point ask any close friend or relative of a person who suffers with depression. Their response will testify to the truth of emotional responsibility, because they most probably have tried many times to make that individual feel better, but with little if any long-term effect. At best, you can only encourage a particular response; the power to create that response rests mostly with the people themselves.

The fear of hurting others also demonstrates little respect for others' ability to handle the discomfort of their own emotions. It disrespects others' tolerance levels, promoting the unhealthy idea that they will disintegrate and die directly from your assertion. This simply is not true: others do have the resources to cope.

In addition, there is another very important reason for you to overcome the fear of others' feeling uncomfortable when you assert yourself. If you hold back and stop assertion in an attempt to rescue the individual from their uncomfortable emotion, that avoidance is a reward for their previous behaviour. Your silence and lack of assertion rewards the way they have treated you. Remember that silence is consent. If you say nothing through fear of their feeling hurt, you have allowed them to get away with it. Do not be too surprised if they treat you in an inconsiderate manner when a similar situation occurs again. Your rescuing them from their responsibility teaches them that they can treat you, and others, how they like, with little if any consequence. That is why we strongly recommend emotional responsibility – it not only encourages you to be assertive but also teaches others how you wish to be treated.

If you accept the principle of emotional responsibility then the fear of hurting another will diminish. It will subside because you will no longer assume responsibility for their emotions as well as your own. You will accept that their hurt belongs to them to deal with, just as your frustration belongs to you to deal with. We suggest that you hold a healthy belief that reinforces the above points. For example:

> 'I would like this person not to feel hurt, but I have no guarantee they will not. Although uncomfortable, they, and I, can stand my assertion.'

This belief accepts and respects each individual's emotional responsibility. It also draws attention to your tolerance level, reinforcing the healthy idea that assertion will not kill you or them. In addition, it respects others' ability to cope with their uncomfortable emotions.

One caution: overcoming the fear of hurting others does not give you carte blanche so that you can be nasty to others and then, when they feel hurt, say to yourself, 'Nothing to do with me. They hurt their own feelings.' Assertion means respecting the feelings of others, so although you won't take responsibility for any hurt the other person feels in response to what you say, you will take full responsibility for what you say and how you say it. Therefore when you assert yourself you choose to do so respectfully.

Overcome the idea that others know what you want

Unhealthy belief: 'People must already know what I want without my having to ask them.'

This irrational belief works on the premise that others can read your mind without your having to say a word. It is based on the vain hope that the other person will surmise exactly what it is you desire just by your body language or changes in tone of voice. This fuels passivity and aggression. It fuels passivity as it encourages you to stay quiet and not express exactly what it is you want. This passive approach temporarily avoids the discomfort of speaking up. The only problem is that the other person is not telepathic. What you assume they absolutely should have deduced from your subtle hints, they may have completely missed. It may not only be that they have missed your subtle hints, but your passivity may also invite them to dismiss easily whatever it is you think they must do. In addition they may misinterpret your behaviour, coming to an inaccurate conclusion: e.g. your partner personalizes your bad mood, assuming that you are offended with him or her. The above belief promotes passivity in that you stay quiet, expecting them to respond to your subtle cues. The other person may not be aware or may be resistant to your request, hence they do nothing and you remain dissatisfied with the situation.

The irrational idea that others absolutely should know what you want without your having to ask them also fuels aggression. It does this by relying on your rigid standards that you believe others should automatically follow and obey. For example, John rigidly believed that his partner did not need to be told exactly how he felt, but that she should deduce this from his behaviour. As already noted, John's relationship was progressively deteriorating because he would regularly become unhealthily angry when his partner did not respond to him sympathetically on his return home from work. On assessment, he explained that he would often come home from a day's work feeling tired and irritable. On arriving home his partner, who had also been working all day, seemed to show little regard for his irritated mood. She seemed preoccupied with her own interests and did not prioritize John's desires. Instead of openly relaying his emotions and wishes, he would sit in front of the television going over the thought, 'Why is she not responding when it is plainly obvious that I have had a bad day?' This then triggered a rigid unhealthy belief:

'She absolutely should know that I want her sympathy.'

At this point John would become increasingly angry at his partner's seeming lack of regard. This fuelled further silence that frequently resulted in an explosion of accusations of how she was always thoughtless and uncaring. John learned in therapy that to stop an angry outburst he would be better off intervening far earlier. He confronted the irrational idea, dispelled the notion that she was telepathic and openly communicated his desires. Eventually John got so proficient at this that on more than one occasion he telephoned his partner before leaving the office, briefing her on a particularly bad day and requesting sympathetic treatment when he arrived home.

We encourage you, like John, to challenge and change the unhealthy belief that people should absolutely know what you want without your having to communicate this to them. We recommend that you change the above belief to a more realistic healthy alternative. For example,

'It would be nice if they knew, but they do not have to. It is worth tolerating the discomfort of speaking up, as there is more chance of my desires being met if I do.'

This belief accepts that there is no reason why others should telepathically know what you want. It also encourages you to assert your desire early. This thwarts unhealthy anger at the seeming insensitivity of those you are attempting to reach.

Overcome the idea that you must have an easy life

Many of us have wasted time hoping something will magically happen without us having to act. This is fuelled by the mistaken notion that maximum happiness can be achieved by doing very little, if anything, yet still accomplishing a lot. Reality does not endorse or support this passive approach to life. Getting your desires met easily with little hassle will only happen occasionally. What seems to be the case is that it takes work, and lots of it, to be consistently heard and for others to respect you.

If you demand an easy life and attempt to avoid hassles, you will have a tendency to experience more discomfort and disappointments in your life. This may seem too ironic to be true, but there are two reasons we believe this to be the case. First, your demand leaves you over-sensitive to life's hardships and hassles. To illustrate this point, think of how many red cars you have seen today. Perhaps only a few, if any? The reason for this is because you were not looking out for them. Now imagine that this morning you heard on the news that a terrorist organization had planted a bomb in a red car somewhere in the country. How many would you have noticed? Probably many more. Why? Because you were looking out for them as they now pose a threat to your security or comfort zone.

This illustrates how demanding that life be hassle-free leaves you more sensitive and hypervigilant to potential hassles and discomforts. Additionally, by holding the demand, you may also exaggerate how bad these events will be if they occur and underestimate your ability to tolerate them when they do occur. Therefore, you notice more potential hassles, overestimating the hardship to your life if they happen. If, then, you hold the unrealistic rigid belief that 'life must be easy and hassle-free', you will be hypervigilant to problems, inferring there is more potential hassle and hardship in your life than there really is. You may also exaggerate the hardship and discomfort far more when hassle occurs.

The second reason for this belief fuelling more hassles is the unhealthy behaviour it encourages. Demanding an easy life with no hassle encourages you to assume that assertion is just not worth all the aggravation. The easiest way of handling the situation is to avoid confrontation altogether. This can create a vicious cycle for you. The reason for this is that people learn from you how you wish to be treated. Respect is seldom automatic. Individuals learn how you wish them to behave, through your making clear what you find acceptable and unacceptable. If you choose to ignore someone behaving indecently towards you, that goes to reward his or her behaviour. Remember, silence is consent, so that if you say nothing, others learn that they can get away with it in the future. Therefore, we get the behaviour from people that we are willing to put up with without protest.

Although assertion is at first uncomfortable, initially perhaps even making things worse for you, in the long run you are more likely to get the behaviour from individuals that you desire.

We suggest that to overcome this unhealthy belief you hold the following healthy alternative:

> 'I would like life to be easy but I am not immune from hassles and discomfort. Although assertion is temporarily uncomfortable, the long-term benefits outweigh the short-term gain of avoidance.'

We believe that this healthy philosophy encapsulates flexibility and the reality of life's hassles. In addition, it promotes tolerating the temporary discomfort of assertion, highlighting a good rationale for doing so. The healthy belief leads to more motivation, encouraging you to intervene earlier. This thwarts uncomfortable assertion tasks piling up, possibly leading to an easier life where others learn quicker how you wish to be treated.

Overcome the urge to keep your feelings to yourself

Terence Rattigan wrote that our greatest vice was 'to refuse to admit to our emotions. We think they demean us.' This quote encapsulates how some of us view our emotions, as something to be repressed or kept confidential. George held this rigid rule that we 'absolutely should' keep our feelings to ourselves. This illogical belief led him to make unhealthy conclusions about expressing how he felt. For example, here is a selection of George's unhelpful conclusions that he held while believing the above rigid demand:

'Because it is rude for me to express my emotions.'
'Because it is embarrassing to say how you feel.'
'Because I may overwhelm or burden my family, and that would be a horrible thing to do.'
'Because they may reject me if I am honest about what I am feeling.'
'Because it is weakness on my part to express my emotions.'

George agreed that his unhelpful conclusions would only be reasonable if he were emotionless and just functioned mechanically like a machine. Yet this is simply inconsistent with the human experience. We are emotive beings and we are designed to feel and express those emotions. It is prudent therefore to challenge your ideas about expressing emotions if you have a habit of holding back. The reason for this is that the consequences can be unhealthy if you continually deny this essential part of your make-up. In our practice, we have seen a number of people who over a long period of time have denied their emotions. They have also refused to express their feelings to others, and this is fuelled by one or more of the fears cited above. These individuals have subsequently suffered from intense anxiety, depression and shame, and quite often physical complaints, such as high blood pressure.

The irrational idea that we must keep our emotions to ourselves is illogical because we do experience emotions every day. George tried to keep his emotions strictly to himself and he became increasingly dissatisfied in his relationships, thinking no one understood him. His family viewed him as distant and detached, and this had a detrimental effect in their interaction with him. As a result it became increasingly more likely that George bottled up his unhealthy emotions. This eventually led to his experiencing explosive outbursts where he inferred he had lost complete control. In addition, these unhealthy outbursts were usually not directed to the member of his family that he had an issue with; more often they were vented at someone or something less threatening to him, i.e. a close friend or housemate.

To overcome the unhelpful belief that you absolutely should keep your feelings to yourself, we suggest a more realistic philosophy that accepts the human condition. For example, George found the following belief far more realistic:

> 'I would prefer not to experience this uncomfortable emotion, but being human essentially means I will experience it. Although it's hard to assert myself, it's not going to kill me, and it will help in the long run if I do express how I feel.'

This belief encouraged George to express how he felt at the time he was experiencing it. In addition it encourages the understanding that showing emotion is part of being human and that the effects are rarely as disastrous as you may have previously thought. It also prevents the long-term consequences that can result through repressing and denying your emotions.

Summary

The aim of this chapter has been to provide you with a clear set of motivations for fostering assertion. We have highlighted eight principles that we hope will encourage you to look after yourself and others in a more healthy, balanced way. This list of principles outlines the main components of a framework for healthy interaction in relationships. We then highlighted seven common unhealthy beliefs that may be underpinning your fear of assertion. This section suggested how you could challenge and change these unhealthy beliefs, thus removing any obstacles that may have been blocking your assertion.

In the next chapter we will show how you can question and flush out the unhealthy beliefs underpinning your aggression or passivity.

3

Learn to identify and question your unhealthy and healthy beliefs

Before you can be assertive it is necessary to be in the right frame of mind. If you are not in the right frame of mind you will quickly sabotage your assertion skills by falling back on aggression or passivity. Therefore it is important to be skilled at questioning your unhealthy and healthy beliefs before, during and after your assertion. Questioning your unhealthy and healthy beliefs will help to reinforce your new healthier philosophy, thus making it more likely that you will stick to your assertion even when the going gets tough.

In this chapter we mainly focus on how to question beliefs that fuel aggression. We will do this by teaching you three lines of enquiry that you can use to flush out any unrealistic, illogical or unhelpful thinking. We then go on to highlight how John (introduced in the first chapter) used the questioning process to remain assertive instead of falling back on his aggressive way of communicating. In this chapter we also include further skills you can use to deepen your conviction in your new healthy beliefs. Finally, we conclude with a summary of the questioning process and why it is so beneficial. Before reading this chapter, it would be helpful for you to review from Chapter 1 the four different components of unhealthy and healthy beliefs. To help refresh your memory we have briefly summarized them in a list below:

Unhealthy beliefs are defined through:

- rigid demands;
- awfulizing;
- low frustration tolerance (LFT);
- self/other depreciation.

Healthy beliefs are defined through:

- flexible preferences;
- non-awfulizing;
- high frustration tolerance (HFT);
- self/other acceptance.

Three lines of enquiry to aid you in questioning your beliefs

The goal when questioning your beliefs is threefold. First, you need to realize that your unhealthy beliefs are clearly unhealthy; second, you need to understand the healthy alternative to the unhealthy beliefs; third, you need to realize why the alternative beliefs are themselves healthy. To meet this threefold goal you need to convince yourself through forceful reasoning, questioning both the unhealthy and healthy alternative. The reason why both beliefs need to be questioned is that it is important not only to contradict the beliefs underpinning your aggression, but also to confirm the beliefs that go to underpin your assertion. There are three lines of enquiry that aid you in evaluating your unhealthy and healthy beliefs. These are in the form of three questions:

- Is this belief going to help me?
- Is this belief in line with reality?
- Does this belief make sense?

These questions show up the futility of holding your unhealthy beliefs and reinforce the value of your healthy beliefs. Forceful questioning will weaken your conviction in the beliefs that underpin your aggression or passivity, and strengthen your conviction in the beliefs that underpin your assertion. To illustrate: if you wish to have a picturesque garden, it is important not only to pull out the weeds, but also to plant and tend the flowers. You would not just pull out the weeds and plant nothing in their place, because this would leave your garden looking bare. In the same vein you would not plant flowers without removing the weeds first, as the weeds would eventually choke out the flowers. This illustrates how it is important to uproot the unhealthy beliefs that underpin your aggression or passivity. At the same time it is necessary to bed in through the questioning process the healthy beliefs that will fuel your assertion.

Let us now see how John applied these three questions to the four beliefs that lay at the core of his aggression.

How John learned to question his beliefs

Using John's example we will give a step-by-step guide to questioning the beliefs that underpin aggression. We encourage you as we do our clients to write down your responses to the questions, as this adds clarity and will serve to help you focus on what you are thinking.

You may recall that John is a 31-year-old man who works as a stockbroker. He found that he had a very short temper with people and that while his anger was effective in getting people to do things for him, it was detrimental to his intimate relationships. John explained that he wanted to be able to get closer to people, especially his girlfriend, who found his angry outbursts very difficult to handle. John explained further that his girlfriend had threatened to leave if he did not find some way to 'control' his anger. John had also occasionally hit out at inanimate objects during arguments with his girlfriend.

Let us now show you how John used the questioning process to uproot his unhealthy beliefs and convince himself of his healthy, more rational beliefs.

Rigid demand:

'I must prove I am right, and she is wrong.'

Question:	Is this belief going to help me?
Answer:	No. This is the very belief that fuels my aggression and leads me to communicate poorly. It also fuels rumination which can keep me in a mood for hours, even days.

Question:	Is this belief in line with reality?
Answer:	No. There is no law stating that my partner must always agree with me. If there were such a law she would automatically agree with me on everything. The very fact that she does not, on more than one thing, highlights the lack of evidence to support my unhealthy belief.

Question:	Does this belief make sense?
Answer:	No. It does not make sense to expect that everyone, however near and dear, will agree with me all the time. We all have our own opinions and to demand that she must see things my way does not follow on at all.

Awfulizing:

'If she does not accept that she is wrong and I am right it will be absolutely horrible.'

Question:	Is this belief going to help me?
Answer:	Only if I want to remain aggressive in my communication. I am clearly exaggerating this bad event and making it into an end-of-the-world catastrophe. This may well threaten our relationship so it does not help me at all to think of her disagreement as 'absolutely horrible'.

Question:	Is this belief in line with reality?
Answer:	No. It is obvious to me that her not accepting my decision is not the worst thing that could happen to me; therefore it is obviously not horrible.

Question:	Does this belief make sense?

Answer: No. It is bad for me that she has not accepted my decision, but it does not make sense to say it is 'horrible'. For something to be horrible it would have to be 100 per cent bad, the very worst that could happen. It is obvious to me that logic dictates there has never been anything in the history of man that has been 100 per cent bad. Therefore I accept that this situation could be a lot worse, so it does not make sense to believe this is the very worst that could happen to me.

Low frustration tolerance (LFT):

'It's intolerable that she thinks she is right and I am wrong.'

Question: Is this belief going to help me?
Answer: No. As I have noted, this belief leads to aggression, and that leads me to speak and act in a way that I later regret.

Question: Is this belief in line with reality?
Answer: No. I am stating that her not accepting my decision is intolerable. If that were true then I would die when she did not accept my decision, but this is obviously not the case. I can stand it, therefore this belief is not consistent with reality.

Question: Does this belief make sense?
Answer: No. It does not follow that something that is uncomfortable is intolerable.

Other-damnation:

'Damn her for not seeing it my way.'

Question: Is this belief going to help me?
Answer: No. Damning my partner for not agreeing with my decision is at the root of my aggressive communication style. It is this belief that has led me to lash out at inanimate objects during arguments. It only helps me if I want to stay aggressive with her, and consequently jeopardizes my relationship.

Question: Is this belief in line with reality?
Answer: No. There is no evidence to back up the notion that a human being can be damnable because of one act or thought. Additionally, if it were true that she actually was damnable, then there would be nothing good about her at all; this is certainly not the case.

Question: Does this belief make sense?
Answer: No. It does not make sense to rate her totally on one act or decision. It is just not logical that a human being can be completely evaluated on the basis of one aspect.

We encourage you to apply the above questioning process to the unhealthy beliefs that you identified as underpinning your aggression or passivity. Writing out your response to each question, as John has done, will not only be an aide memoir, but will also help clarity of thought. As we noted earlier, after uprooting your unhealthy beliefs it is necessary to deepen your conviction in your healthy beliefs. You are now ready to apply the three questions to your alternative beliefs that underpin your assertion.

Flexible preference:

'I would like her to see it my way, but there is no law stating she has to.'

Question: Is this belief going to help me?

Answer: Yes. This belief will encourage me to be assertive when I feel healthy annoyance at my partner for not agreeing with my decision. It will also go to benefit us as a couple, as I will not attempt to enforce my opinions when she does not agree with me.

Question: Is this belief in line with reality?

Answer: Yes, since I am not demanding that she must act a certain way (demanding something that is external to my control). My preferring that she acts in a certain way is in line with reality as it allows for flexibility: sometimes she will agree and other times she will not.

Question: Does this belief make sense?

Answer: Yes. This specific belief follows my general preference that I like people to agree with my decisions, but as I have found out many times, they will not always agree. This makes logical sense as it follows on from my general experience.

Non-awfulizing:

'It's bad when she thinks she is right and I am wrong, but hardly the end of the world.'

Question: Is this belief going to help me?

Answer: Yes. This belief allows me to be healthily annoyed and assertive when my partner does not agree with my decision. Since I am acknowledging that it is bad, I am able to remain proactive in the face of her disagreement. This aids my assertion and reasoning skills, allowing me to make my point satisfactorily.

Question: Is this belief in line with reality?

Answer: Yes. I can provide lots of evidence to support this belief. For example, it is bad when my partner does not agree with my decision as it will most probably inconvenience me, but an inconvenience is hardly a catastrophe. I cannot, on the other hand, provide any evidence to prove that it is an end-of-the-world tragedy when she does not agree with my decision. Therefore the evidence points to my healthy belief being in line with reality.

Question: Does this belief make sense?

Answer: Yes. It is perfectly logical to view a bad event as bad, and not to exaggerate it into some end-of-the-world tragedy.

High frustration tolerance (HFT):

'Although uncomfortable I can stand her thinking she is right and I am wrong.'

Question: Is this belief going to help me?

Answer: Yes. This belief helps me because it fuels healthy assertion and not unhealthy aggression.

Question: Is this belief in line with reality?

Answer: Yes. It is true that I find it uncomfortable when she thinks she is right as I would like her always to agree with me. I can, however, stand her disagreeing with my decision and I will get over her disagreement; therefore it is uncomfortable, but hardly intolerable.

Question: Does this belief make sense?

Answer: Yes. It follows logically that it is uncomfortable for me when my partner disagrees with a decision I have made.

Other-acceptance:

'She is not completely damnable for thinking she is right and I am wrong. I fully accept her as a fallible human being who is made up of many aspects, and this is only one aspect of her.'

Question: Is this belief going to help me?

Answer: Yes. By accepting my partner as a complex human being who cannot legitimately be valued totally on one decision or action, I remain accepting of her and stop damning her as a person. By accepting her I remain assertive and do not try to enforce my point aggressively. This keeps our communication respectful and healthy.

Question: Is this belief in line with reality?

Answer: Yes. The evidence shows that my partner has the potential to

57

agree and disagree with any of my decisions, thus highlighting how complex and changeable we are. No one decision or action typifies her whole being, therefore she cannot be totally damnable for not agreeing with me on this one occasion, just as she is not totally acceptable when she has agreed with me on other occasions. My healthy belief is perfectly in line with reality.

Question: Does this belief make sense?

Answer: Yes. It makes sense to believe that my partner is fallible for not agreeing with me. It is also logical to assert that she is complex and hence will not always agree with what I think is right.

Further skills you can use to deepen your conviction

To really grasp your healthy beliefs that will go to underpin your assertion, you will need to deepen your conviction in them. By deepening your conviction in them there is more chance that your healthy beliefs will affect the way you think, act and feel. There are several methods you can adopt to do this; we will highlight two of the most common ones used in Rational Emotive Behaviour Therapy (REBT). They are:

1 forceful healthy self-statements;
2 rational-emotive imagery (REI).

Before we highlight these two methods of deepening your conviction, please note: it will take a long time and a variety of methods for you to integrate your new healthy beliefs consistently and make them your own. For human beings to change the way they think, act and feel in a consistent way requires persistent hard work. If you expect to make profound life changes just through questioning your beliefs, you will be sadly disappointed because it is not that easy. You will need to keep practising your new healthy beliefs for some time, using the methods we have shown you, before a profound shift occurs. Don't let this discourage you, though: you can change and it is well worth the effort when you do.

Let us now highlight how you can use two methods mentioned earlier to reinforce further your healthy beliefs leading to assertion and weaken the unhealthy beliefs that lead to aggression or passivity.

Forceful healthy self-statements

One way of reminding yourself of the beliefs that will fuel your assertion is to write them down on a small card (about the size of a credit card) and carry them around with you. Then, at opportune times, go over them forcefully in your head. The reason we emphasize 'forcefully' is that it is important to fight fire with fire. Your unhealthy beliefs may have been in place for many years: they are going to take real force to be uprooted. Therefore, if you forcefully go over your healthy beliefs, reminding yourself of your written responses to the three questions cited above, you are reinforcing change through repetition. It will then be easier and come more automatically to you to recall them when you need to be assertive.

John did this and found it very helpful. He wrote down his healthy belief that led to assertion on a card. He went on to highlight the significant words that he would give emphasis to when practising his belief. His cue card read as follows:

> I would like her to see it my way, but there is no law stating she has to. It's bad when she does not see it my way, but hardly the end of the world. Although uncomfortable I can stand her thinking she is right. She is not completely damnable for refusing to see it my way. I fully accept her as a fallible human being who is made up of many aspects and this is only one aspect of her.

First, John practised his healthy belief out loud in a forceful, dramatic manner. Second, he practised his belief to himself over and over again: when he was going into work, when he was at work, while in the bathroom – in fact, whenever he had a moment – out came his cue card. In this way he supported his conviction in his new healthy belief.

Rational-emotive imagery (REI)

REI is a method of deepening your conviction in your healthy beliefs by using your imagination.[1]

Instructions

1 Close your eyes and imagine that you are back in the situation where you communicated aggressively or passively. Imagine this event as vividly as you possibly can. As you do so, try to make yourself feel as unhealthily angry or as anxious as possible. Do this by rehearsing the unhealthy belief that you identified as underpinning your aggression or passivity.
2 Then, while still imagining this event as clearly and as emotively as you possibly can, change your unhealthy anger or anxiety to healthy annoyance or concern by practising the healthy belief that underpins

---

[1] There are two versions of REI. For a full discussion on the other version and on other methods used to deepen your conviction in your healthy beliefs, see Windy Dryden, *Reason to Change: A Rational Emotive Behaviour Therapy (REBT) Workbook* (New York: Brunner-Routledge, 2001).

your assertion. Keep going over the healthy belief forcefully until you no longer feel unhealthy anger or anxiety, but feel healthy annoyance or concern.

3 Practise this for at least twenty minutes a day for at least the next two weeks.

This method is very effective as it gives you the opportunity to engage your imagination and your emotions, which serves to deepen your conviction.

Here is how John practised his REI:

> I closed my eyes and imagined myself sitting at the table where my partner was rejecting my decision. While seeing her do this in my mind's eye I practised the unhealthy belief that led to my aggression, allowing myself to feel unhealthy anger towards her. Then while still holding the image of her disagreeing with my decision, and experiencing some unhealthy anger, I changed my unhealthy anger to healthy annoyance and became assertive. I did this by forcefully going over my healthy belief on my cue card. I continued to go over my belief until I experienced a real shift in my emotions and could vividly see myself being assertive.

John resolved that he would practise REI every day for ten minutes in the morning and ten minutes during his lunch break at work. He did this for two weeks.

Summary

It is worth noting that our aim in this chapter has been to aid you in your intellectual understanding of your healthy beliefs. This is not all that is required to fully adopt your new healthier philosophy. Along with intellectual understanding you will also need to work on emotional understanding of your new healthy beliefs. That is why many of our clients tell us, after questioning their unhealthy and healthy beliefs, 'I know that my healthy belief is true [intellectual understanding], but I don't *feel* it is true [emotional understanding].'

Therefore, just knowing your healthy belief is true will not be enough to give you that deeper conviction required to make profound life changes. To make those profound changes you will need to do a lot of work on weakening your conviction in your unhealthy beliefs while in the situation in which you were previously aggressive or passive. Persistent action is required to gain emotional understanding.

Let us use an illustration to explain this final point. Imagine that you go to your local GP for a check-up. She expresses concern about your cholesterol level, and goes on to advise you that it can be controlled through your diet. You review together the evidence to support her diagnosis, and also the results to your health if you do not give up eating unhealthily. You leave her office totally convinced intellectually that a new healthy-eating philosophy is the best option. On leaving the practice you go over the preferable foods in your mind, reinforcing your new resolve. At lunch you go straight to the local burger bar and order a portion of fries and a cheeseburger. Although you *know* (intellectual understanding) that it won't help your cholesterol level, your actions go to reinforce your old unhealthy-eating philosophy. As a consequence you are more likely to feel (emotional understanding) that your old unhealthy-eating philosophy is true, because your action will go to support your unhealthy beliefs about eating.

When you visit your GP again for another test, your new healthy-eating philosophy alone will not have been enough to shift your cholesterol levels. To make a profound change to your health you will need to combine healthy thinking and action. The same is true with the healthy beliefs that underpin your assertion. Even though you have intellectual understanding it will not be enough to deepen your conviction in your new healthy belief unless your actions are in harmony with your healthy thinking. Therefore the intellectual understanding that can be gained using the questioning skills from this chapter will need to be reinforced with action. Then through questioning combined with action you will not only have intellectual understanding, but also over time you will feel that your new belief is true (emotional conviction). Once you combine intellectual understanding with action and then gain emotional understanding, you will stick to assertion and not fall back on aggression or passivity.

In the next chapter we will show how you can assert yourself by using specific assertion skills.

4

Specific skills in assertion coaching

In this chapter, we will highlight six core skills that will start you off in your assertion coaching. Just knowing these skills will not automatically mean that you will be assertive. Like any skill training, it will take practice for you to feel comfortable with your attempts at assertion. We advocate frequent use of these skills, as this will encourage a more natural and proficient delivery. We do not suggest that you have to be perfect in the way you employ these skills. Practice will only improve your use of them rather than making you perfect. In conjunction with these specific skills you will benefit from combining the healthy thinking that we identified in Chapters 1, 2 and 3.

After considering each skill in turn, and our suggested sequence of their use, we will reinforce the skills and sequence with a table at the end of the chapter. If you wish, you can photocopy this table and use it as a flashcard to prompt and remind you during your initial attempts at assertion.

Preparing your case

Preparation is not always possible as some interactions require immediate assertion. If appropriate, however, we recommend taking a brief time to prepare your case. The reason for this preparation is that forethought will add to the fluency of your delivery, which in turn will add to your confidence.

We suggest that this process of preparing your case be done on paper. Writing your case down adds to clarity of thought and contributes to the structure of your delivery. This will add to your focus and decrease the chances of going off on unfruitful tangents. Our suggested format when preparing your case is as follows. We assume that you have already used your healthy thinking skills and are feeling a healthy negative emotion in the situation under consideration.

Identify which healthy negative emotions you felt in the situation

These may be sorrow, annoyance, disappointment, sadness, concern, etc. We think it is important to acknowledge your healthy negative emotions honestly in an episode. The reason for this is that suppressing or avoiding your emotions is not healthy. Research seems to indicate that swallowing your emotions and not expressing them constructively leaves you vulnerable to stress-related illnesses. Headaches, tiredness, digestion complaints, breathing difficulties, to name just a few, have all been linked to stress or anxiety. Acknowledging and then expressing your healthy negative emotions appropriately will lead to healthier living for you and contribute to your experiencing improved relationships.

Identify what it is about the situation that you did not like or agree with

Identifying specifically what it was that you did not like or agree with will help you to keep focused in your assertion. It will also help in reaching a compromise, as you can accurately convey what it is that you want to change. If you have trouble identifying exactly what it was that you did not like, use our magic question:

> 'If there was one thing that I could have taken away from that situation which would have stopped me feeling ... [*state identified emotion*], what would it have been?'

We have found that this usually yields an accurate appraisal of what it is you specifically do not like and want to change.

Plan your proposed compromise

As we have already stated, assertion promotes a win–win situation. When preparing your case, consider a compromise that the other individual would also agree to. When doing this, consider a shared goal that encompasses equality and concession from both sides. This will increase the chances of your proposed compromise being accepted. Allow scope for change in your planned compromise, as this will give the other person opportunity to give suggestions. Avoid preparing a compromise that has no leeway. Enforced compromises that are presented as set in stone trigger the idea that you are attempting to manipulate or control the situation or the other person. This in turn will lead them to accept your compromise grudgingly, only to resent the agreement – and you – later.

Consider key words you plan to use when asserting yourself

At this point you can decide which words you may wish to use when asserting yourself. This is important, as certain misplaced words can prompt the other person to become defensive. When selecting specific words to use, avoid sarcastic, tactless or defamatory words. Instead, choose constructive, considerate and encouraging words as these will go to create a positive environment for your assertion. We do not recommend that you write down your assertion verbatim, rehearsing it exactly word for word. This will make your assertion sound as if you are reading from a manuscript, and will go to stifle your natural flow. We recommend instead that you keep certain key words in mind and then decide where you wish to place them. These key words will aid in building up the skeleton of what you wish to say.

Choose when best to have your meeting

Choosing the meeting time not only has your interests in mind but considers the other party. The time for the meeting is best negotiated with the other person, but will most probably be instigated and suggested by you initially. It is easily done, just by asking:

> 'I have something that I would like to discuss with you. Is now a good time?'

Be flexible with the person, but be careful not to be put off for too long, as the individual may be avoiding you because of their fear of confrontation. If you receive a negative response initially, enquire when a good time will be. For instance:

> 'I accept that you're busy at the moment, but when would be a good time?'

In summary, to prepare your case:

1 Identify the emotion you experienced.
2 Identify specifically what it was that you did not like or agree with.
3 Plan your proposed compromise.
4 Spend some time considering the key words you wish to use when asserting yourself.
5 Decide when best to have your meeting.

Let us briefly illustrate how to prepare your case with a situation that Denise experienced. Denise had bought a garment that did not measure up to her expectation when she had returned home and tried it on again. Her written preparation looked like this:

---

1 Identify the healthy negative emotions you felt in the situation:

Very disappointed and annoyed.

2 Identify specific aspect of the situation that you did not like, or agree with:

Disappointed with quality of garment, annoyed that I now have to take time out to return it.

3 Planned compromise:

First option, that garment is replaced, or second, that money be refunded.

---

4 Key words I plan to use when asserting myself:

'Feel disappointed, unsatisfactory quality of garment, want to return and have replaced.'

At this point she decided which key words she wished to use if she met with resistance:

'Not receiving satisfactory service, complaint to manager, annoyance at wasted time.'

Denise planned a few final words if her assertion effort was still ignored:

'Very disappointed, unacceptable treatment, name address head office and managing director.'

Remember, the above is only a framework, not a manuscript. It serves as a reminder, for which you can make a mental note.

5 Choosing the best time to have your meeting:

Going midweek when it is quieter. This will benefit me, as I will hopefully get undivided attention, and benefit the retail staff, as they will not be overwhelmed by customer demand.

Preparation does not mean sitting on a situation that you are unhappy about, and putting off your assertion. It does what it says: prepares you to take assertive steps now. Preparation does not need to be a lengthy process – you are better off keeping it brief. The reason for this is that initially the longer you leave your assertion the more time you have to get yourself worried about what may or may not happen. This may lead you to underestimate your ability to handle things assertively, worrying about how you will cope with the other person's possible response. Consequently the longer you leave your assertion the worse your worry gets. When finally you assert yourself, your worry will be so high that you may be too nervous to focus on what it is you are trying to say. For this reason, we advocate early intervention because it deals with matters quickly and efficiently. The quicker you assert yourself, the less time you have to make yourself worry.

We will now explain the skills that you can use during your assertion. We have placed these in the sequence we believe you will initially use them. This does not mean that you will only use each one once during one particular assertion: you may have cause to use the same skill a number of times.

We will now highlight how you can make your point clearly, without being unduly distracted. The skills that will help you do this are focus and repetition.

Focus and repetition

Many people will deflect your assertion using the unhealthy skills of avoidance and counter-attack. Focus and repetition will keep you and your assertion on track and will be a protection from others distracting you. In your preparation, you would have decided what specific point you are making and what your preference is for the future. To focus during your assertion, be clear, following the structure cited above: i.e. emotion first, what it is that you do not like or agree with, and your suggested compromise. Make your point simply and succinctly. Remain brief, avoid adding extra information that will only cloud or obscure your specific point. Then employ repetition, stating exactly what you said previously. For example, George was afraid that if he kept repeating his point he would sound like a broken record. Yet in practice he found that repetition served as a way of focusing his father on the main point he was asserting. It also helped George relax, as he knew that he would not have to keep thinking of new things to say during the assertion.

What if someone raises an issue for discussion while you are asserting yourself with him or her? If the other person does bring up something they want to speak about with you, you could say,

'I can see that's important for you to speak about with me, and I am more than happy to discuss it with you at a later date. The point, though, that I have approached you about is this . . .'

Then refocus the discussion, repeating yourself if necessary. This will keep your main point in focus and will aid in its being remembered.

In summary, focus and repetition assist you in making your point clearly and succinctly. This aids the recipient of your assertion in remembering exactly what your wish or preference is. Keeping focused on the specific point and constantly bringing the other person back to your main point will reduce tangents that often result in fruitless arguments. Keeping it simple and brief stops your listener becoming overwhelmed and confused by a torrent of too much information. This contributes to the point you asserted being remembered exactly.

Listening skills

For your assertion to reach its objective, listening skills are vital. Remember, assertion promotes equality, and has as its target a win–win situation. To attain this goal, you will need to be attentive in following what others' suggestions, opinions and emotions actually are. We will highlight how you can do this by using good body language, active listening to facilitate others expressing themselves, and good following skills to keep people communicating.

First, let us highlight some good body language that will convey your interest and receptivity to others' ideas, opinions and emotions.

Good body language

As we have pointed out in previous chapters, a considerable amount of information about ourselves is conveyed through our body. Our facial expressions, movements and posture can signal an invitation to someone that we want them to communicate with us, and that we are listening. Poor body language can have the adverse effect, shutting down communication. We will now list in sequence some body language techniques that will add to your listening skills:

Forward posture

When the other person starts to respond to your assertion, it is helpful to lean forward slightly. Leaning forward signals your interest in what the other person has to say. In addition, leaning forward indicates acceptance of the individual, and shows you have a high regard for their contribution to the matter. A word of caution, however: be careful not to invade an individual's personal space. This is an aggressive gesture and can construct an uncomfortable environment for the individual.

Open posture and gestures

When the other person starts to respond to your assertion, we suggest you keep your arms and legs unfolded. An appropriate open posture suggests that you are relaxed, non-judgemental and open-minded to the other's suggestions. In addition, be conscious of your gestures; keep them slow and rhythmical. If possible mirror the other individual, as this shows that you are following very closely what they are saying. An additional technique is to nod while the other person is responding to your assertion in a positive or neutral way. If they start to give a negative response, or one that you do not like, do not shake your head in disagreement, as the other person may become defensive in response. Instead, stop nodding and perhaps hold your chin in a pensive, thoughtful pose.

Eye contact

Looking directly at the person responding to your assertion indicates you are concentrating and concerned with what they have to say. It demonstrates that you are genuine and honest in your regard for their contribution to what you have previously asserted. Your eye contact, however, does not have to be constant; brief periods of focusing on their mouth or hands and arms would also be appropriate. Yet the large percentage of your gaze will preferably be to their eyes.

Appropriate smiles

A smile placed at the appropriate time can give a very positive message to the other person. It signals approval and warmth, and can be used to show your agreement with what the other person is saying. Smiles, however, need to be handled and placed with precision and care. If wrongly placed they can be misread and the other person may respond aggressively, since they may think that you are humouring their contribution. Smiles can be hazardous if you have identified a passive approach to communication. Actually we suggest that if you have identified passivity, avoid smiles at first. They can be misinterpreted and used as a disqualification of what you have just asserted. The point to remember is: use a smile as a signal that you agree or are happy with the outcome.

This concludes the section on body language to reinforce your listening skills. We will now identify how you can employ active listening skills.

Active listening

Many people falsely believe that listening is passive, where you sit and do nothing. We believe this not to be the case. Skilful listening is an art form that encourages others to open up. We will now point out some skills that you can use to be able to be active in your listening. These are not in sequence, as you may refer to different listening skills throughout your interaction.

Verbal prompts

Verbal prompts are the 'mm-hmm' and the 'oh . . . really' interjections. They constitute minimal following sounds that highlight your intent in hearing the other person's view or suggestion. They are not interruptions but are a gentle encouragement that invites the other person to continue. Verbal prompts emphasize that you are following what the other person is saying.

Open questions

Open questions cannot be answered with just a 'yes' or 'no', they require further information. Asking open questions encourages someone to voice their opinion, decision or emotion. It can also persuade someone to continue to reveal what he or she is thinking or feeling. Examples of open questions are:

'How do you feel about that now?'
'In what way did you want it changed?'
'What is it that you have decided to do?'

A word of caution: we have included 'open questions' in active listening as they are to be used to keep the person talking, and for you to encourage open, honest communication. For this reason avoid difficult or over-personal questions, because the other person may respond with defensiveness, as they may infer that you are interrogating them. In addition keep your questions to a minimum, for, as we will highlight, allowing for silence is also an active listening skill.

Reflecting

Reflecting is a very important element of communication. The reason for this is that so many disagreements are based on an initial misunderstanding. When reflecting you can use three methods: reflecting content, reflecting emotion and reflecting possible reasons.

Reflecting content is when you repeat what has been said. For example: 'So are you saying that you are not too bothered that you turned up ten minutes late to our appointment?' Here you capture the essence of the content of their response in your own words. This gives the other person the opportunity to hear what they have said, and for you to check out whether you heard it correctly.

Second, you can reflect the emotions that the other person may be experiencing, mirroring back clearly and simply what you suppose they may be feeling. For example: 'It seems to me that you are feeling annoyed – is that true?' This will encourage the other person to express their emotions to you, hence giving you more of an honest response.

Third, you can reflect back possible reasons, connecting triggers with emotions. For example: 'So is it that you felt hurt when I did not say goodbye?'

Notice all the three reflective skills are always pitched as a question. This is to avoid sounding like a psychologist or detective, diagnosing why you think the person has acted or feels a certain way.

Reflection skills serve to facilitate an open and honest communication, where you get a true understanding of what the other person is thinking or feeling. Why not try to employ just one of these reflective skills in your everyday conversation and see if it increases the effectiveness of your listening skills?

Thoughtful silences
Silences need not fill you with dread or be actively avoided. They can be used to your benefit. Allowing some silence gives the other person time and space to consider your assertion, and then to think and formulate a response to you. Further, it demonstrates your confidence in yourself and what you have asserted. To confirm this last point, notice when someone talks a lot without allowing you to get a word in. You most probably interpret this as nervousness or that the other person isn't interested in what you have to say. A thoughtful silence coupled with good eye contact (see p. 68, 'Eye contact') will send out the message, 'I believe my opinion is sound and worthwhile,' and 'I am interested in what you have to say.'

In conclusion, you will most probably have to practise these listening skills many times for them to become a natural component of your interactive style. Just trying them out, though, will most probably have great effect on your assertion and relationship skills. Other people will be more comfortable talking to you and will be more open and less defensive in your company. Active listening conveys the message that you value that individual's opinion or emotions, creating an environment where others want to express themselves to you.

Communication skills

Being a good communicator and avoiding 'defence triggers' will add to successful assertion. Defence triggers are styles of communication that can spoil our interaction with others. They are best avoided because they can trigger your listener's defences, with the consequence that they distance themselves from you. We will now highlight eight potential 'defence triggers' to avoid:

1 name-calling;
2 psychoanalysing;
3 manipulative praise-giving;
4 judging;
5 prescriptive advice-giving;
6 closed questions;

7 unrealistic reassurance;
8 changing the subject.

Name-calling

This is a common and easy trap to fall into. It is especially tempting to engage in name-calling when starting to become unhealthily angry or hurt. It requires you to stereotype and then label the person as a whole. For example:

'You are a complete waste of space.'
'You're just another self-centred man who is a total idiot.'

Name-calling is one sure-fire way of derailing your assertion, leading to an argument. Remember, the best way to win an argument is to avoid it happening in the first place. Name-calling is a sign of defensive aggression that considerably lessens the chances of a win–win finish.

Psychoanalysing

Psychoanalysing, as used here, means imputing negative motivation to people's behaviour, which tends to put them on their guard. Sharing your diagnosis of why you believe someone responds or behaves in a certain way to you can be a catalyst for an argument rather than constructive communication. Examples of psychoanalysing are:

'Just because you have been promoted you think you're so important.'
'Your problem is that you believe you're God's gift.'

This can immediately alienate you from the person with whom you are being assertive. We encourage holding back on giving a prescriptive opinionated reason as to why you think someone is responding in a certain way. If you think that it is appropriate to share your view, we recommend avoiding the closed psychoanalysing approach, where your listener has no say in your diagnosis of them. Instead, we suggest that you employ 'reflecting back reasons', as this gives you an opportunity to voice your view while also allowing the other person an opportunity to contribute (see pp. 69–70, 'Reflecting'). By the way, our use of the term 'psychoanalysing' here has nothing to do with psychoanalysis as a form approach to psychotherapy.

Manipulative praise

Manipulative praise constitutes false commendation or compliments that are meant to make it hard for the other person to say 'no'. They come in the form of

'Be a good lad and . . .', or
'You know you're such a helpful lady, you wouldn't mind . . .'

71

The other person may respond with resentment to this form of manipulation and they may become resistant to what you have to say.

Judging

Others will not respond favourably when you sit in the judgement seat and tell them what you believe they should or should not have done. Their most likely response is irritation and resentment. To avoid the pitfall of judging, be careful not to say things like:

> 'You really shouldn't have ...', or
> 'You ought to ...'

Being someone else's conscience and adopting the moral high ground will alienate you from them.

Prescriptive advice-giving

Prescriptive advice-giving is similar to judging, but goes one step further. With prescriptive advice-giving you tell the person directly what you believe they should do. For example:

> 'I think you ought to ...', or
> 'If I was in your shoes, I would have ...'

This spoils good communication as it undervalues the other person's problem-solving skills or coping ability.

Closed questions

Closed questions are questions that require only one-word answers. They are assumptions that close off another's opportunity to comment, such as:

> 'You must be so angry?'

Closed questions only require a 'yes' or 'no' answer and do not credit the individual with the respect of being able to identify their own opinions, emotions or actions. As a result, closed questions do not foster open communication.

Unrealistic reassurance

Unrealistic reassurance can sound very patronizing. It relies on weak assumptions from you that have no real evidence. The goal of unrealistic reassurance is to give a quick fix to an individual's problem, with the aim of lessening the emotional intensity that the individual is experiencing. For example:

> 'Don't worry, everything will be all right,' or
> 'I am sure that it will all turn out for the best.'

Where is your evidence for such predictions? The truth is, we usually have none. This kind of reassurance is unhealthy as it is used to withdraw from the emotion being experienced.

Changing the subject

Changing the subject has a similar goal to unrealistic reassurance. It is used to move away from the uncomfortable emotions being experienced. For example:

'Let's talk about something positive,' or
'Don't worry about it, let's talk about what you did enjoy.'

Changing the subject is a poor communication skill. It may well highlight a fear of intense emotions that will stifle your receptivity to others and stifle their openness with you in response to your assertion.

The above eight 'defence triggers' are only a summary of many communication styles that could spoil your attempts to be assertive. To work on your communication skills try to be objective. Why not review your communication skills by examining your conversations to see if you can notice any possible 'defence triggers'? In addition, if you perceive someone becoming defensive with you, use that situation to your advantage to see what has triggered his or her response. This feedback can be done tactfully just by asking,

'I notice just now you seem to have changed. Have I offended you?'

This can yield good comments that you can work from.

In conclusion, there are many ways that we can set up a trigger for others' defences. We are better off if we are mindful of what we have a habit of saying that may act as a defence trigger for others. By our recognizing and changing these unhelpful communication styles, the other person may be less resistant to change and more open to us. As assertion strives for equality, then, our endeavour to keep the lines of communication open is vital. On occasion, though, people will throw in comments as a way of diverting your assertion. They may even attempt to throw some accusations at you as a means of distraction. How can you handle this effectively? By using agreement and requests for specific examples.

Using agreement and requests for specific examples

Agreement and negative enquiry are two excellent assertive techniques. Employing agreement and requesting specific examples can mean that your assertion does not degenerate into an argument. You use these skills to ensure that you briefly respond to the other person but you keep the focus on what you want to say.

Agreement is a response for you to use when someone raises something about you that is true. The point they raise may represent a weakness or trend of unhealthy behaviour that you have displayed. Agreement is an acceptance of the observation with an acknowledgement and ownership of that particular personality or behavioural trait. Simply put, agreement means that you assert

'Yes, your observation about me is true.'

Calmly agreeing with their true criticism of you shows your self-confidence and removes any friction that could result in an argument. Hence, your assertion remains on track, removing their attempted distraction.

Requesting specific examples is a response for you to use when someone raises something about you with which you do not agree. Here, you request specific occasions when you have presented that weakness, or displayed the trend of unhealthy behaviour of which they have been accusing you. Simply put, requesting specific examples is a further investigation of evidence before you accept their observation. This form of assertion will clearly indicate whether the person is offering a constructive opinion or is aggressively attempting to trigger off hurt in you. If they are sincere, then their highlighting this negative trait will help you and improve your relationship with them.

To illustrate the use of agreement and requesting specific examples, imagine that you wanted to be assertive towards your partner. Let us suppose that you have noticed that they seemed preoccupied of late, spending more time in secular pursuits than with you. You feel sad at their seeming lack of regard and wish to draw this to their attention. In preparing your case, you decide to offer a compromise of more time together this coming weekend. While you are highlighting your partner's apparent lack of regard and how you feel about it, your partner throws in a point that you have faltered on: for example, 'Well, at least I don't overspend on the credit card.'

This statement is a red herring, a comment intended to distract attention away from your assertion. How do you handle it without getting sidetracked into pointless argument while losing your original focus? This is where agreement and requesting specific examples come in. If there is truth to this comment, then agreement will keep your conversation on track. For example, you may simply reply,

'I accept that I have a tendency to overspend on occasion,'

and stop there. Agreement is not a justification of your weakness, for that would hand over control to your partner. Nor is it intended for you to put yourself down, with your partner thinking they have the upper

74

hand. Agreement is a confident acceptance of your fallibility. It removes the fuel for an argument and has the ability to stop people in their tracks. You would then most probably choose to revisit the skill of focus and repetition, repeating exactly what you had said before they raised their negative comment.

What if you believe their negative comment is not true? Then you could request a specific example. For example, your partner retorts, 'Well, at least I don't overspend on the credit card.' If there is generally no truth to this comment then requesting specific examples will keep your assertion on track. For example, you may reply,

'That is interesting. When specifically have I overspent on the credit card?'

and again stop there. This question is intended to smoke out their true intentions. If it is a genuine and valid criticism, then they will be able to cite some good examples of this occurring. If their comment is constructive then remain objective, taking what they say on board and accepting that we all have weaknesses and failings.

Our suggestion is, then, to use agreement at the points they raise which are true. We also encourage you not to start talking about the point they have raised – leave that for another time. Perhaps make a point of assuring your partner that you will broach this issue on another occasion. For example, once they have cited some good specific occasions, you could comment,

'I accept that on the specific occasions you mentioned I have overspent on the credit card [agreement]. If this issue is important for you to speak about with me, I am willing to discuss it with you later. The point, though, that I have approached you about is for us to spend more time together this weekend [focus and repetition].'

In summary, agreement and requesting specific examples are tools to keep you from being thrown off course by counter-comments from the person to whom you are making the assertion. These two assertion skills indicate your self-confidence in handling constructive criticism healthily, while still enabling you to assert your point.

Appropriate self-disclosure

Self-disclosure is a skill that encourages you to share how you are honestly feeling. It has a twofold purpose. First, it allows you to be honest with yourself and others in expressing your emotions or thoughts during your assertion. Second, it is a great bridge between people, helping your listener to identify with you and not see you as a distant figure who cannot be trusted.

In practice, we suggest keeping your self-disclosure brief and simple. The reason for this is so as not to confuse or bore the person to whom you are making your assertion. With this in mind, avoid irrelevant padding to your self-disclosure. Only offer a general emotion or thought about the situation. We suggest stating the emotion first and the trigger for the emotion second. For instance:

> 'I felt nervous speaking about this with you, as I did not want you to feel hurt,' or
> 'I have been concerned about the way you treated me, and have been giving it some thought.'

Being succinct is effective, as your listener does not get distracted with irrelevant detail.

Why is self-disclosure such an effective assertive skill? Quite often people can relate to you more after you self-disclose. They can see that you are reachable and not some emotionless, distant figure. Self-disclosure is also non-threatening, encouraging someone to trust you more than he or she did previously. This will create an environment where there is a sense of trust. Your candid honesty will hopefully invite the other person to be more comfortable when being open with you, as self-disclosure tends to be reciprocated.

At what point do you use self-disclosure? We believe self-disclosure can be used at any point in your assertion. You can start your assertion with it, insert it in the middle, or even end your assertion with it. Using self-disclosure at the beginning of your assertion is a great way of reducing your initial anxiety. For example, you may begin by saying:

> 'I feel nervous mentioning this because I cherish our friendship and do not want you to think I am being critical of you, but ...'

Self-disclosure in the middle of your assertion provides a good example for the other person, making it easier for them to be honest with you. For example, you may say:

> 'I am interested in your response to what I have just raised, because I value your opinion.'

When closing your assertion with self-disclosure you promote equality and encourage a healthier relationship. For example, you may finish with:

> 'I am glad that we could have this frank discussion. I am pleased with the outcome.'

In conclusion, attempt to self-disclose at least at one point in your assertion; it builds bridges and helps your listener identify with you.

Negotiating a realistic compromise

'Peace can only be achieved by understanding,' said Albert Einstein. To negotiate a realistic compromise, attempt to understand and take into consideration the desires, suggestions and emotions of both parties. This is not an easy task as everyone is individual in their likes and dislikes. A realistic compromise cannot be too heavily weighted in your favour or in that of the other person. A careful consideration of each other's wishes is necessary for a compromise that will be agreeable and workable. When discussing a compromise, keep in mind that you are just as important as the other person. In addition to that, remember that it is possible to have two winners if you carefully construct a mutually acceptable plan of action.

How can you do this effectively? Simply consider a compromise where you give 50 per cent and they give 50 per cent. To do this skilful preparation may be required. This is so that you can have some suggestions in mind for discussion. Then when asserting yourself, use listening skills to encourage honest communication of what you both would see as a desired outcome. Allow the other person time to voice their preferences. Discuss the personal factors involved for each of you, and then consider the feasibility of your proposed compromise from both your standpoint and that of the other person. Include time constraints, and finally promote flexibility as it is rare that a compromise is executed perfectly.

Colin put this structure into good effect. As mentioned earlier, Colin is the managing director of his own company; he and his partner Liz work in the same office together. On occasion, Liz would highlight Colin's failings in front of the staff. This was a source of irritation for Colin. After working through his blocks to assertion, we negotiated a compromise that was realistic and workable. Colin then asserted himself with Liz and they both decided that Liz would stop highlighting his failings in front of the staff. They then considered that, given the stress triggered by the job, it might be hard for both of them always to hold back.

Colin and Liz negotiated a 'time out' policy, so that if either of them wanted to raise an issue, they could retire to a spare office where they would privately work it through. To allow for time constraints and flexibility Colin and Liz discussed an alternative. They both decided that if it was a particularly busy day, implementing the 'time out' policy would not be practical. The alternative was a note system where Liz or Colin would hold the information back until the end of the day. They would then conduct a meeting where feedback would be given, and improvements to their individual approaches discussed without the staff listening in. They both practised this to good effect. Their working relationship improved and Colin also maintained the respect of his employees. Because they settled matters quickly during the day, Colin and his partner enjoyed a better relationship outside of the office. This is a good example of a balanced, realistic compromise where both parties were catered for.

In summary, when negotiating a compromise with the person you wish to be assertive towards:

1 Clarify your desired outcome – what you want your goal to be.
2 Investigate what the other person's goal is, giving the other person the opportunity to contribute to what they think the desired outcome should be.
3 Consider equality in your compromise. An effective way of doing this is by asking yourself whether you would accept your compromise if you were in that person's shoes.
4 Be mindful of each other's time constraints. Ask yourself whether there is sufficient time to action the proposal thoroughly.
5 Make room for flexibility. Take into consideration each other's fallibility by accepting that your proposed compromise will not be carried out perfectly.

After considering all of the above skills, you should have enough of a skill base to start practising assertion. As we have pointed out at the beginning of this chapter, you will need to practise these skills to become proficient at them. Many of our clients find it rewarding and stimulating when they begin to employ these skills in their everyday conversations, as well as when they are specifically being assertive. We warmly encourage you to do the same; you have nothing to lose and everything to gain once you become adept at using your assertion skills.

Table 4.1 summarizes the sequence of assertion skills highlighted in this chapter. You may photocopy this and use it as a flash card to prompt and remind you during your initial attempts at assertion. It has been designed to be placed in a bag or pocket for easy and discreet reference.

SPECIFIC SKILLS IN ASSERTION COACHING

1 Prepare your case by:

a identifying your emotions
b identifying what you did not like or agree with
c planning your proposed compromise
d deciding which key words you plan to use
e choosing when best to have your meeting.

2 Focus on your listener and repeat your point

3 Use these listening skills:

a good body language
b open posture and gestures
c eye contact
d appropriate smiles.

4 Be active in your listening:

a employ verbal prompts ('Hmm . . . Oh really . . .')
b use open questions (How? What? Why? When?)
c use reflection ('So you are saying . . .?')
d allow for thoughtful silences.

5 Communication skills to avoid:

a name-calling ('You lousy . . .')
b psychoanalysing ('Your problems is . . .')
c manipulative praise ('You're great, would you . . .?')
d judging ('You really should not have . . .')
e prescriptive advice giving ('If I were you . . .')
f closed questions ('You must be angry . . .?')
g unrealistic reassurance ('Don't worry')
h changing the subject ('Let's not dwell on it').

6 Agreement and negative enquiry

a agreement ('That's true, I do . . . at times')
b requesting specific examples ('When have I . . .?').

7 Appropriate self-disclosure

8 Negotiate a realistic compromise

a be clear about your desired outcome
b investigate the other's goal
c consider equality in your compromise
d bear in mind time limits
e be flexible, allowing for fallibility.

© Professor Windy Dryden & Daniel Constantinou, 2004

5

Assertion of positive emotion

Most of us enjoy receiving gifts, especially when they are given genuinely and without condition. When we do receive such gifts, it can engender a feeling of warmth, knowing that our contribution has been appreciated. Actually, there has been a wealth of psychological research on how we respond to receiving gifts, most of which highlights our enthusiastic response when receiving them, because we perceive gifts as a reward.

Gifts do not always have to be something tangible, like a watch or some perfume. That is why there is the phrase when receiving a gift that 'it is the thought that counts'. In our communication with others, we can give rewards in the form of genuine, unconditional verbal gifts. These personal expressions of positive emotion go to acknowledge the other person's contribution. These verbal gifts are assertion of a positive emotion. What is assertion of a positive emotion, what is its benefit, how can it be used and when is it appropriate to employ this type of assertion? We will answer all these questions in this chapter, but first let us define what we mean when we encourage assertion of a positive emotion.

What is assertion of a positive emotion?

Assertion of a positive emotion is your verbal expression of an emotion about a specific contribution that someone else has made. It is a brief, honest acknowledgement of your appreciation or recognition for what that person has said or done. It is not a contrived statement motivated by selfish gain; rather, it is a verbal gift given unconditionally. An example of asserting a positive emotion is:

'When you telephoned and expressed concern for me, I really appreciated it. I find your thoughtfulness refreshing.'

or

'I respect your resourcefulness and performance on this project.'

These are not lengthy, over-the-top expressions; rather, they are succinct and realistic.

What are the benefits of asserting a positive emotion?

Assertion of a positive emotion has a similar function to the assertion discussed previously. It serves to teach people what you like and do not like. Where the assertion already discussed highlights what you do not like, assertion of a positive emotion points out what you do like. Consequently, it serves to teach the other person how best to treat you, aiding them to learn from their successes as well as from their failures. This increases the likelihood of their repeating the positive contribution that you enjoyed. There are two reasons why they are more likely to repeat what they have said or done after you have acknowledged their contribution. First, they know you like what they have said or done. Second, they have received a verbal gift which acts as a pleasurable reward for them.

To reinforce this definition of what assertion of a positive emotion is, and to highlight what it is not, see whether you think the following six statements are true or false:

1 Assertion of a positive emotion encourages people to relax their standards and start taking it easy. *True or false?*
2 People only do better when you point out their mistakes. *True or false?*
3 People automatically think that you are after something when you offer a positive comment. *True or false?*
4 Assertion of a positive emotion is always embarrassing and uncomfortable for both parties involved. *True or false?*
5 Offering a positive comment is soft and weak. *True or false?*
6 People should know they have done well without my having to tell them. *True or false?*

In fact, *all* of the above statements are false. They constitute wrong assumptions about asserting a positive emotion. To dispel these false assumptions, let us briefly discuss each one in turn.

Statement 1 falsely maintains that asserting a positive emotion encourages people to relax their standards and to start taking it easy. Assertion of positive emotion does not do this; indeed, quite the contrary. We believe it serves as a learning curve for the individual receiving it, as it underlines what your standards are. In addition, the person has received a reward, which more often than not serves as a motivator to repeat what they have done.

Statement 2 puts forward the false assumption that people only do better when you point out their mistakes. We do not believe that assertion of a negative emotion is the only way to teach someone. For example, think about a time when you have worked hard on a project.

How did you feel when your partner or boss merely highlighted what you did *not* do instead of also acknowledging what you did well? You were most probably demoralized and despondent. We believe that asserting a positive emotion is just as effective as asserting a negative emotion in that it encourages people to act, or treat you, in a way that you find acceptable.

Statement 3 assumes that people automatically think you are after something when you offer a positive comment. We have observed this not to be the case every time someone engages in asserting a positive emotion. Not everyone concludes, 'What is she after?' Suspicion about your motives largely depends on the person receiving your assertion and how they personally perceive it. If someone is wary of your assertion of a positive emotion, it may be due to his or her mistrustful view of people in general. Time will reveal your true intentions. If you know through experience that someone is suspicious of others, then avoid making requests in the same discussion as the one in which you assert a positive emotion. This will teach them that your assertion is honest and offered unconditionally.

Statement 4 claims that asserting a positive emotion is always embarrassing and uncomfortable. Any embarrassment and discomfort that you may first experience will soon dissipate the more you realize that there is nothing shameful or threatening about offering positive affirmation. Practice increases your fluency, and will improve your confidence in your delivery. Remember, it does not have to be long-winded – just a few well-chosen words will be sufficient.

Statement 5 wrongly maintains that asserting a positive emotion is soft and weak. We believe quite the opposite. The reason for this is that it shows strength of character to voice your opinion and view. To remain quiet and not say anything often highlights passivity. Being honest and sharing your emotion, even when it is a positive one, does not display weakness: rather, it displays confidence in your observations.

Finally, Statement 6 wrongly asserts that people automatically should know they have done well without your having to tell them. This is false, unless of course they are telepathic, in which case they will be able to read your mind and know that they have done well. If you wish people to perform repeatedly to a standard you find acceptable, then the direction and guideline given in asserting a positive emotion will point the way for them. By believing 'they should already know', you will decrease the possibility of their behaving in that acceptable or helpful way again. If you wish them to repeat what you liked, let them know.

In summary, assertion of a positive emotion is a verbal gift given unconditionally that teaches the other person what you find acceptable.

It is not a contrived, exaggerated expression that is given for some kind of selfish gain.

How can you identify whether you are asserting a positive emotion correctly and not being aggressive or passive when delivering what you have to say? We will answer this question in the next section.

How to assert a positive emotion

The expression of a positive emotion is used to give information to people about useful comments or actions that they would do well to repeat in the future. To aid you in knowing how to use this form of assertion effectively, we will highlight characteristics that would be evident when employing it. We will also contrast asserting a positive emotion with aggression and passivity, both of which are unhealthy and are best avoided. First, how to identify healthy assertion of a positive emotion compared with unhealthy aggression.

Asserting a positive emotion with aggression

We will now look at three ways of communicating that would indicate aggression rather than healthy assertion. Characteristics of aggression while engaging in positive assertion are as follows.

Asserting a positive emotion sarcastically

If the assertion of a positive emotion is given in a sarcastic manner, this would denote aggression. For example, when offering a positive emotion without sarcasm, you might say:

'Thank you for preparing that meal, it was delicious. I really enjoyed it.'

Contrast this with a positive emotion given in a sarcastic tone:

'Oh, what a really delicious meal, someone must have helped you prepare it.'

The latter is not assertion of a positive emotion at all, but is intended to put the other person down. Sarcastically minimizing their achievement serves to elevate you over the other person. This is unhealthy as it does not promote equality.

Asserting a positive emotion grudgingly

Another aggressive characteristic is asserting a positive emotion grudgingly. For example, when offering a positive emotion without resentment you might say:

'I am delighted with your decorating job, it has a real professional finish. We will use you again.'

In contrast, offering the same positive emotion grudgingly may sound like this:

> 'Well, I suppose it's not a bad decorating job, I am reasonably happy with it. Let us just say you got there in the end.'

This form of asserting a positive emotion is aggressive, as it gives with one hand but takes with the other. It does this by disqualifying the positive affirmation, implying you do not really mean what you say.

Asserting a positive emotion with excessive praise

In addition to asserting a positive emotion sarcastically and grudgingly, there is also excessive praise-giving. This is aggressive, as it is manipulative and patronizing. For example, appropriate positive assertion is brief and to the point:

> 'I am encouraged by your motivation when teaching your children.'

In contrast, the same assertion with excessive praise-giving would be over the top. For instance:

> 'I am thrilled to see the way you are with your children, you really are the greatest mother.'

The latter is excessive and can sound very insincere and patronizing. The main problem, though, is that the receiver usually disqualifies excessive praise, as they do not really believe what you are saying. Consequently, it is not effective in encouraging a repeat of the specific word or action you are drawing to their attention.

The three aggressive traits we have highlighted are asserting a positive emotion sarcastically, resentfully or with excessive praise. We believe these approaches are unhealthy, because they can sound artificial and condescending. Consequently, your assertion of a positive emotion may be disqualified, resulting in the person being less likely to repeat the way they acted. Asserting a positive emotion can also be adulterated by passivity. We will now highlight two passive traits that would indicate unhealthy assertion.

Asserting a positive emotion with passivity

Characteristics of passivity while asserting a positive emotion are as follows.

Asserting a positive emotion with an apology

When asserting a positive emotion it would be done without apology. For example:

> 'I was pleased with the way you handled that person, you were firm, but fair.'

This contrasts with offering the same positive emotion passively. For example, when offering the same emotion passively you would say:

'I hope you don't mind me saying, but I was pleased with the way you handled that person. I am sorry if I have spoken out of turn.'

Apologizing for offering your observation disqualifies your opinion. This highlights an inferiority complex, which left unchecked will adversely affect all your interactions with people.

Putting yourself down while asserting a positive emotion
When asserting a positive emotion in a healthy manner you might perhaps say:

'I welcomed that presentation, I appreciated all your preparation.'

This contrasts with offering a positive emotion with a self-putdown tacked on at the beginning or at the end. For example:

'I welcomed that presentation, I would never be able to talk as well as that.'

Here your aim is to elevate the other person above yourself. This is not promoting equality; rather, you are downing yourself to raise others.

The two passive traits we have highlighted are asserting a positive emotion apologetically, and putting yourself down during your assertion to the other person. Both these approaches are unhealthy, as you are elevating others at the cost of denigrating yourself. Remember, all healthy assertion promotes equality in worth. We are all equal regardless of how well you believe someone has or has not performed. We encourage you actively to avoid passivity when asserting a positive emotion. To continue to elevate others at the price of putting yourself down will lead to feelings associated with a sense of low self-worth.

When to assert a positive emotion

Asserting a positive emotion should preferably be employed with discretion and tact. Some occasions benefit from this form of assertion, yet in some circumstances it can be counter-productive for you. The occasions when it is beneficial are too numerous to mention specifically. The principle to remember is: assert a positive emotion when you perceive it will have a learning function for the individual and will go to benefit your relationship with them. This can be at home, at work, in a social setting, in a meeting or anywhere you see fit.

Knowing when not to engage in asserting a positive emotion depends on your experience with the individual concerned. For example, beware of someone repeatedly responding to your assertion by constantly disqualifying what you have said with negative information about themselves. This would indicate that asserting a positive emotion is having minimal impact as they are invalidating your comments. For example, they may say:

'It was nothing, don't mention it, you should have seen my first attempt.'

This indicates a sense of low self-worth which will cause the other person to be adept at disqualifying positive feedback with negative information about themselves. This way of thinking renders asserting a positive emotion meaningless. In contrast, if when offering a positive emotion the other person agrees, and then adds to what you have highlighted, proceed with caution. This kind of response would indicate that they have an unhealthy, egotistical view of themselves. An example of this is someone replying to the effect:

'Yes, I agree, I did do well. What can I say? I always do a good job.'

They are using your assertion as a booster to their already inflated ego. They will misinterpret your assertion of a positive emotion, falsely believing it is further evidence that they are superior to others.

Both negative responses to assertion that we have just discussed indicate that your assertion will need to be used with great tact and skill if repeated in the future with such people. Incidentally, the healthiest response from someone following your asserting a positive emotion is simply a 'thank you'. This indicates that your positive assertion has been received in a healthy manner.

Using the assertion sandwich

Start off your communication with an assertion sandwich. What we mean by this is saying something positive to a person, then asserting a negative feeling, and then ending on a positive note. An assertion of your negative feeling is literally 'sandwiched' between two positive statements. We suggest you use the assertion sandwich (a) when you are dealing with someone quite fragile, and (b) when what you have to say is quite negative and needs to be put into a balanced context. Here is an example of how Joan used the assertion sandwich with a friend who would monopolize conversations. Her assertion went like this:

'I relish your company, because I think that we agree on a lot of issues [*assertion of positive emotion*], although sometimes I am disappointed because it seems to me that we spend most of our time speaking about you and what you have done [*assertion of negative emotion*]. I would prefer it if we could share the conversation [*suggested compromise*]. The reason that I raise this is that I cherish our friendship and want it to last [*assertion of positive emotion*].'

This worked to good effect, as the friend had not realized that she was doing this. In addition, Joan's personal expressions about their friendship served as a healthy motivational influence on her friend amending her conversational style. The reason for this is that the assertion sandwich decreases the chances of the other person becoming defensive. Hence, they remain open to your negative assertion. This skilful use of assertion is not approval-seeking, it is decency in action.

A cautionary note: we encourage discretion when using positive assertion sandwiches with people who tend to be aggressive, as they may choose to use it in disqualifying what you are asserting. Colin used a positive assertion sandwich with a particularly difficult member of his staff. His goal in the assertion was to make the point of punctuality, as this staff member had been perpetually late over a number of weeks. Colin started his communication by asserting positively the emotion he felt when he observed the standard of work this staff member regularly achieved. He then made it clear that although the standard of the employee's work was good his punctuality was poor at present, and this would need to be addressed immediately. The staff member disqualified Colin's assertion of a negative emotion by aggressively excusing his behaviour using Colin's initial positive assertion. On reflection, Colin wished he had simply asserted a negative emotion. This illustrates how those who tend to lean towards aggressive communication styles can use your positive assertion as ammunition in disqualifying what you are negatively asserting.

Summary

Asserting a positive emotion can work for you as effectively as asserting a negative emotion. If used appropriately, it is a potent force for encouraging people to repeat behaviour you enjoyed. As an experiment, why not observe a friend or family member and assert a positive emotion which is accurate and thoughtful. Then measure their response and see if it improves your relationship and fosters a repeat of the favourable behaviour. We believe that it will.

6

Adapting your assertion to the person

We would always encourage you to tailor your assertion to the specific person you are dealing with, as inappropriately delivered assertion can trigger a self-protective response. By understanding an individual's way of interacting, you can make your assertion more palatable by adapting your style to the specific person. Realistically it is not always possible to do this, and sometimes you cannot avoid someone deciding to become defensive. We do believe, though, that if you can become proficient at ascertaining the person's style of interacting, then you can reduce the chance of a poor response and increase the chance of a successful outcome for both of you. In this chapter we will teach you how to become proficient at ascertaining what type of communication style is being employed by the individual you are being assertive with. In this way, you can adapt your assertive style to the individual. Before doing that, we will discuss the core principles that underpin healthy relationships, highlighting how to establish and maintain healthy boundaries in all aspects of your life. We will conclude this chapter by describing five different communication styles.

First, we will explain how to establish and maintain healthy boundaries in all your relationships.

Why healthy boundaries lead to enduring relationships

While travelling in the countryside you come across this sign: 'Keep Out, Trespassers Will Be Shot, Then Prosecuted.' What do you do? The foolhardy may press on, but the large majority of us will heed the warning and avoid the cordoned-off area. Ask yourself, would I have kept going if there were no sign and no consequence? The answer is most probably 'yes'! Without boundaries being made clear, and where there is no penalty for trespassing those boundaries, it is unlikely we will stop ourselves. This principle also applies to our interaction with other people. When we assert and maintain healthy limits to what we will put up with, even with our nearest and dearest, it leads to a respectful, enduring relationship.

To illustrate, let us return to Joan's example. For as long as Joan could remember she had been verbally 'pushed around' by her husband. He would try to control her, and seemed to take delight in putting her down when in the company of their friends. When Daniel enquired about how she responded to her husband's putdowns, Joan shrugged her shoulders and said, 'I am usually so embarrassed that I either stay quiet or do what he tells me to do.' Joan set no boundaries with her husband, so he thought he was entitled to trespass and control all aspects of her life. This led him to disrespect their relationship and perpetually treat Joan like a doormat. It will come as no surprise that Joan wanted Daniel to work on raising her low self-esteem.

Please ask yourself this question: who taught Joan's husband to treat her this way? She did! Although it was painful for her to admit it, Joan agreed that she had never asserted her boundaries. This meant he did what he pleased, believing there were no consequences to his actions. In effect, Joan had allowed him to treat her that way, never setting the parameters to their relationship. He trespassed with no penalties. In fact, her responding to his behaviour the way she did rewarded him and so he learned to use it repeatedly. In their work together Daniel taught Joan an assertive technique that helped her regain respect from her husband.

After some work on her fear of rejection, Joan was able to implement the following technique with great success. This assertive technique not only created healthy boundaries in her relationship, but also served to maintain a healthier view of her self-worth. This approach to instigating healthy boundaries was first put forward by our colleague Dr Paul Hauck in 1997. It is a structured way of implementing boundaries and stopping others treating you like a doormat. We will now explain how you can implement this technique in your life.

Implementing and maintaining healthy boundaries in your relationships follows a similar structure to the player rules in rounders or baseball. You may recall that you are given three attempts to hit the ball; on the final attempt if you miss you are struck out. We encourage giving individuals two chances to change their unacceptable behaviour that trespasses on your boundaries. On each of the two occasions you assert your preference, giving the other person a chance to change their action and improve your relationship together. This is like the first two chances in baseball; you get two attempts with no penalty implemented. On the third occasion, you unangrily implement consequences that are just as uncomfortable as what they have done to you on the previous two occasions, having stated previously that you are going to do this.

You may think this is a little harsh, but what is the alternative? The alternative is that you do nothing and the person will, in all probability, keep on treating you badly. The reason for this is that if someone does not respond to two assertive attempts, and persists in their unhealthy behaviour, it is a trend in their personality. They will continue to trespass on your boundaries, as this is a habit that they have formed and will not break easily, unless they have a reason to. Assertion with no action will not be enough to get them to change their behaviour and save your relationship. For you to establish respect, you are going to have to make their environment uncomfortable so as to get your message through, otherwise they will not stop the inconsiderate behaviour. We believe that creating an uncomfortable environment shows fellow feeling, as its aim is to save your relationship. In addition to this it also teaches the individual how to treat others better.

We are not encouraging like-for-like retaliation: two wrongs do not necessarily make a right. The behaviour you choose has to be just as uncomfortable as they are doing to you, but not at the same level. Remember, the aim is to re-establish healthy boundaries, not destroy the relationship altogether. That is why we advise that when you implement your penalty it should neither be illegal nor cause direct physical injury to the person, nor should you do it angrily. For example, if a colleague at work has been publicly derogatory about your performance on a project you are both working on, you may on the second occasion warn them that if they repeat this for a third time you will make a formal complaint to your manager. You are not lowering yourself to throwing insults back. Rather, you are establishing a penalty that preserves your dignity and also sets clear uncomfortable consequences if your colleague continues to trespass on your boundaries.

Let us explain this further with another example. Imagine that a friend is repeatedly late for appointments with you. On the first occasion you may say:

> 'You know, Ted, I am annoyed that you have kept me waiting for twenty minutes. I would appreciate it if in the future you can get here at the time we had agreed. If that is impossible for some reason, then please could you contact me on my mobile telephone.'

This is setting up healthy boundaries, and if Ted is receptive, your assertion will act as a positive contribution to your relationship, as he will respect you more. It also helps to teach Ted that another's time is just as valuable as his, something that will go to benefit him in all his relationships.

The following week you and Ted have another appointment, and he is twenty minutes late again. Now what do you do? Well, you repeat your assertion, but this time you add on the end a consequence that is just as uncomfortable to Ted as the behaviour he has been giving you. You say:

> 'Ted, I did mention to you last week that I would appreciate it if you could keep to the time we agreed. I am disappointed that you have arrived twenty minutes late again. If you are more than ten minutes late next week then I am going to go on without you.'

ADAPTING YOUR ASSERTION TO THE PERSON

The reason for stating a consequence is that if someone treats you the same way on three separate occasions then this highlights the fact that that particular behaviour is a habit that they will repeat time and time again. Remember, we get the behaviour we are willing to accept without protest. No penalty may lead Ted to believe he can get away with being late without too much discomfort.

When Ted turns up twenty minutes late the following week and finds you have actually carried out what you had stated, he will think twice about repeating that behaviour again. For healthy boundaries to be established you will need to see your action through – that is tough, but think of the benefits to you and also the other person.

Please note, there are two occasions that we do not encourage implementing the above. The first is if your life is in danger, and the second is if you would be financially destitute if you carried out your third strike penalty. First, we do not encourage implementing penalties if your life is in danger. If someone has a knife to your throat, this is not the time to say, 'I find this behaviour highly inappropriate, and if you persist I am going to alert the authorities.' That would not be a wise move. What we encourage is that you get yourself out of the situation by any means you have at your disposal. Once out of immediate danger, you assert yourself and follow through all the appropriate means to seek justice. The second occasion is when assertion will lead to financial destitution. So, for example, your boss is a tyrant and you no longer want to put up with her bullying. Yet your wages put food on your table and pay the mortgage. For this reason you may first wish to make sure you are not financially dependent on that particular job before you carry out your third strike penalty.

As we have already stated, decency permeates all assertion with others. That is why we encourage forethought and consideration of the other person before being assertive. For you to be truly effective in your assertion it is helpful to be able to ascertain the communication style the individual is employing. This not only helps you decide where to pitch your assertion, but it will assist in indicating what kind of penalty is going to be constructive for that individual.

The five communication styles and how to adapt your assertion to each style

Just as you can organize individuals into different blood groups, you can also put into general groups the ways people communicate. We have observed five different categories of communication style:

1 open and chatty;
2 precise and detailed;
3 competitive and to the point;
4 negative and critical;
5 considerate and selfless.

We will now define each in turn and suggest how to tailor your assertive communication to each style.

Open and chatty

This type of person is known as a talker. They love to have others listen to them. In fact, the bigger the audience, the louder, more extroverted they get. They like to make jokes and remain the centre of attention. They have no trouble initiating conversations, and if you are a listener they will be quite happy talking openly for hours about themselves, their view or their friends and family.

When asserting yourself with this type of person, be aware that they enjoy controlling interaction. Avoid being too heavy-handed with them as they like to be liked. This means it will not take too much to get your point across. Do not be surprised if they try to lighten what you have asserted with a joke. They are most probably attempting to regain your approval. If your assertion is one of a serious nature do not let them monopolize the conversation: be brief and to the point. To reinforce the point you have asserted, be the one to initiate the end of the conversation. This will likely require you interrupting them.

Precise and detailed

This type of communicator is switched on by minute detail. They can get over-absorbed in the intricacies of subjects, being fascinated by the logical solution to problems. They can quietly immerse themselves in the detail and precision of subjects and then try to impress you with their 'superior knowledge'. Because of this, they are not great small-talkers; they prefer to discuss the 'nitty-gritty' of subjects they know a lot about.

When asserting yourself with this type of person be aware that they will attempt to go into too much detail with you. This type of person usually has perfectionist tendencies, which means they may see your assertion as a personal attack or criticism. Avoid getting too technical with them, as this will lead you into a fruitless debate. Keep your assertion brief and limit it to just one point; this will inhibit them from getting lost in the detail of your interaction.

Competitive and to the point

This individual will see interaction as a challenge that he or she must 'win'. When communicating they get straight to the point and speak their mind. Their conversation style is very sharp and focused, usually accompanied with a quick wit. They do not have the patience to stomach small talk or tolerate people who talk 'round the houses'. Because of their direct approach they are frequently misread and perceived as insensitive, curt or rude.

When asserting yourself with this type of person, be aware that they will see your interaction as something they 'must win'. They love to argue and are proficient at proving their point, often by exposing the weaknesses of their 'opponents'. They may do this by putting you down during your assertion. They are doing this as an attempt to 'keep on top'. Do not react to their putdown ploys, as they will perceive this as a weakness. Instead, accept that this is their way of dealing with your assertion and shrug off, or if appropriate laugh off, their remarks.

Negative and critical

This type of person would be known as someone who is impossible to please. When communicating they will over-focus on the negative points discussed, always taking issue with the way they think it should have been said or done. They are not only critical of others but also highly critical of themselves. The regular theme of their conversation is how others have done things wrong or how difficult life is for them. They also have a habit of using exaggerated terms, such as 'terrible', 'useless' or 'a complete waste of time'. Negative and critical communicators will be quick to raise objectionable and negative points of view, rarely communicating positive agreement or approval.

When asserting yourself with this type of person be aware that they have a black-or-white view, which means they will see your assertion as either all good or all bad. They will be efficient at filtering out any positive aspects to your assertion and quick to highlight the negative. Negative and critical communicators are quick to highlight your faults as a defence of their already fragile ego. Remember that this type of person can ruminate and go over and over what you have said. For this reason, be brief and well prepared; be careful not to feed their negative view of themselves with a long list of personal issues.

Considerate and selfless

This type of person is known as a listener. They take time to warm up in relationships, at first seeming reserved and self-conscious. They are sensitive to others and can easily take offence. Considerate, selfless communicators are rarely forthcoming with their opinions, as they constantly worry about offending others with what they say and do. They often shy away from confrontation because they fear getting upset in the midst of an argument. Yet, when they trust you, they are usually very loyal and can be a friend for life.

When asserting yourself with this type of person, remember they are particularly sensitive and can easily put themselves down. In your assertion, you will not need to be too forceful in making your point; their selfless approach means that they are particularly concerned about offending you. They will also need more space and time compared to other communication styles to think about what you have asserted, and encouragement to voice their views and opinions on what you have said. Most of all, give them space to think and talk. Avoid interrupting – just listen, and even perhaps encourage them to express their point of view.

Summary

In this chapter we have highlighted how to tailor your assertion to the person with whom you are being assertive. The aim of adapting your assertion is twofold. First, it limits the defensive reactions of the other person. Second, it helps you deliver your assertion appropriately, not being too heavy-handed or too gentle. We have also shown how to construct healthy boundaries in all your relationships. This is by using the three-strike technique. We have shown how this is tough love in action, and can help redeem respect in all your relationships. Further to this, we have classified five different communication styles, and how to adapt your assertion with each one.

In the next chapter we will highlight how you can apply this learning to four specific areas of your life. These are in your intimate relationships, in your friendships, with your work colleagues and with members of the public.

7

Assertion in specific areas of your life

In this chapter we will use the real-life experiences of John, George, Denise and Colin, so that you may learn from their example. We will highlight how they asserted themselves, either in their intimate relationships, in their friendships, in a work environment or with members of the public. This will show you assertion in action.

Assertion coaching in intimate relationships

An intimate relationship is defined by its private and personal nature. It is a relationship with an individual or select few that forges a deep bond with unrestricted expression of affection. Assertion coaching in an intimate relationship is a delicate balance between maintaining intimacy and at the same time not losing your identity. It weighs up and maintains your desire to be close, without relinquishing your sense of who you are and what your individual wishes and preferences are.

You may believe, though, that a successful intimate relationship should not need any boundaries, holding the idea that your partner should automatically not trespass or invade your personal space. We believe this not to be the case. We have observed that healthy relationships are defined through their boundaries. It is true that the boundaries in intimate relationships are certainly drawn closer than in any other relationship setting, but still they are drawn, and at times you will need to highlight them. To keep a relationship healthy, respect for each other is paramount because this creates an alliance between two individuals that is balanced and stable.

John employed assertion coaching in his intimate relationship with his girlfriend, Sue. You may recall from Chapter 1 that Sue had threatened to leave John unless he found some way to 'control' his anger. After some anger management and assertion training, John experienced a situation with his partner in which he would have previously experienced unhealthy anger. John's partner became quite irate at him when for the second time he had forgotten to add her to his private health care policy at work. This presented a potential trigger for John, as previously he would have barked at her, telling her to 'Shut up!' and 'Stop nagging!' and 'Don't you realize what kind of a day I have had at work?' Instead, John recalled his healthy belief: as he felt his unhealthy anger welling up he said forcefully to himself:

'It would be nice if Sue knew exactly what I was thinking, but she does not have to. It is worth tolerating the discomfort of piping up, as there is more chance of my desires being met if I do.'

On this occasion he had not rung Sue previously to notify her how busy his day had been. He paused for a moment before replying to her. He asked if they could continue the discussion over a cup of tea that he would make. While on his own in the kitchen he prepared his case. He also ascertained that, far from her usual 'open and chatty' style, Sue was particularly 'negative and critical' today. John's assertion went something like this:

John: 'I am annoyed that I forgot to put you down on the health care policy at work [*identified emotion*].'

Sue: 'This is the second time I have asked you in a week. What is wrong with you?'

John: 'It is true this is the second time this week that you have asked me [*agreement*]. What I plan to do is to go in tomorrow and to amend my policy first thing [*suggested compromise*].'

Sue: 'Right, and I will telephone you at 11 a.m. to make sure you have done it.'

John's immediate response to this was defensive, as he believed Sue was trying to control him. He stopped himself from becoming unhealthily angry, which in the past would have led to aggressive taunts at Sue. Instead John approached it assertively:

John: 'I understand why you would want to ring me [*reflecting the content of Sue's point*]. I strongly prefer that you leave it to me to remember, and I will sort it out for you tomorrow morning [*repetition of suggested compromise*]. How about this, though: if I fail to do it tomorrow, which is highly unlikely, you can ring me the following day [*negotiating a compromise*].'

Sue: 'All right, but I want you to do it tomorrow.'

John: 'I will do it first thing, before I get distracted as I did today. Now, I notice that you are not quite yourself. Is there anything apart from the health care issue that is bothering you [*open question*]? We do not have to discuss it now, but I want you to know that I am interested if you want to talk [*thoughtful silence*].'

Throughout the assertion John had to fight his previously automatic desire to control Sue through aggression. This would have led him to shout over Sue and perhaps even display his aggression by throwing a few inanimate objects around. Instead, he validated Sue's opinion by listening and acknowledging it; this made his assertion far more persuasive. John found that he reached the same goal as his aggression would have given him, but with the added bonus that his new communication technique strengthened their relationship instead of his aggression weakening it.

George also found that he had to highlight his boundaries in his intimate family relations. This was especially evident in the relationship with his father. After some work on his fear of expressing his emotions he eventually confronted his father, applying the suggestions from Chapter 4. He ascertained where he thought healthy boundaries with his father should preferably be. He then decided that for him and his father to create a healthy relationship he would need to express how he felt about his father's treatment of him. He also observed that his father was a 'precise and detailed' communicator, where he, George, was more 'considerate and selfless'. On one occasion George's father rang him out of the blue. He demanded that George join a mail order club so that his father could receive a free gift for encouraging someone new to join. George did not deal with the issue there and then; he requested some time to think about his father's request and arranged a convenient time to telephone him back. George prepared his case and rang his father as arranged. After pleasantries had been exchanged, the conversation went something like this:

George: 'Dad, I appreciated your call last night, but you know I feel disappointed [*initially George had experienced anger, but on reflection realized that the anger was a cover for hurt*] that you only rang me because you wanted something. You did not even ask how I was, or how work was going [*identifying specific aspect of father's behaviour that George did not like*]. I would really appreciate it if you made more effort to contact me to just find out how I was doing [*suggested compromise*].'

Father: 'But this seemed like such a good offer.'

George: 'Dad, I appreciate that you thought it was a good offer [*reflecting the content of his father's point*], but I would really prefer it if you made more effort to contact me to just find out how I was doing [*repetition of suggested compromise*].'

97

Father: 'But George, I never know what kind of mood you are going to be in. You can seem very distant at times.'

George: 'That's true, I can be distant at times [*agreement*], but I want to have a closer relationship with you now. That is why I felt disappointed [*repetition of identified emotion*] that you telephoned just to ask me to join a club so that you could get the free gift [*repetition of the specific behaviour George did not like*]. I would really appreciate it if you made more effort to contact me to just find out how I am [*repetition of suggested compromise*].'

Father: 'All right, George, I will bear it in mind. Now, how about that introductory offer?'

George experienced a small amount of anxiety when being assertive. He believed he was taking a real risk expressing his emotions, something he had not done before with his father. He faced this fear and came to realize that the worst rarely happens with well-placed assertion. As a direct consequence of George's assertion, his father rang him again a couple of days later to find out how he was, something he had never done before. They spoke for some time on the telephone, communicating more honestly with each other on subjects they had previously avoided. In his final assertion coaching session George testified to the usefulness of being honest instead of avoiding expression of his emotions.

Both John and George's examples highlight the fine balance between maintaining closeness in their intimate relationships and at the same time keeping appropriate boundaries. The above also highlight how assertion in intimate relationships is far more sensitive than in any other setting. The reason why you handle the other person with greater care is because you occupy such an important place in their life. Asserting your opinion and emotions will have a far greater impact, so sensitively delivering your assertion keeps their defences closed and their minds open. Hence the sensitive application of assertion in your intimate relationships means you will establish and maintain healthy boundaries.

Assertion coaching in friendships

A friend can be defined as someone with whom you share mutual interests and whose company you find stimulating. You do not share the intimacy that is characterized by a relationship with a lover or family member, but you have an attachment that fosters a strong concern for each other's welfare. Friends do not occupy the place in your heart that your partner or family may hold, but they are close behind.

Denise asserted her boundaries with one of her closest friends. Denise and Naomi had been best friends for many years; Naomi is 'open and chatty' while Denise identified herself as 'considerate and selfless'. Naomi had recently developed a habit of breaking arrangements at the last minute. Denise was anxious that if she asserted herself she might lose Naomi's friendship. Prior to her attempt at assertion Denise challenged her unhealthy belief that was underpinning her fear of Naomi's disapproval. Denise decided to hold the following healthy belief while asserting herself with Naomi.

'I wish Naomi to like me, and I will even work towards it, but I do not *need* her approval. My thoughts and feelings are just as important as hers.'

Denise decided to test out this healthy belief with some real-life assertion. After ringing Naomi and arranging to meet at a coffee bar, Denise plucked up the courage to be assertive. While at the coffee bar, the following conversation took place.

Denise: 'Naomi, something you did I was disappointed with recently [*identified emotion*], and I wanted to discuss it with you. Is now a good time? You know that I treasure our friendship [*assertion of a positive emotion*], but last Sunday evening . . .'

Naomi: 'Oh, that.'

Denise: 'Well, I was very disappointed that you cancelled at the last minute [*identifying specific behaviour that Denise did not like*]. Now I appreciate that sometimes things will occur that require urgent attention, but this did not come under that bracket. In the future I would deeply appreciate it if when you make an arrangement with me you stick to it [*suggested compromise*].'

Naomi: 'Denise, we just got carried away. We were at the tennis club. We stopped for drinks and before I knew it was eight o'clock.'

Denise: 'I appreciate you got carried away [*reflecting content*], but I was really disappointed [*repetition of identified emotion*] that you cancelled at the last minute [*thoughtful silence*]. I would really appreciate it if when you make an arrangement with me you stick to it [*repetition of suggested compromise*].'

Naomi: 'I am so sorry, Denise. Look, I have my diary now, how can I make it up to you and David?'

Denise: 'Naomi, just work hard for it not to happen again [*repetition of agreed compromise*]. I cherish our friendship a great deal; the trust and loyalty we have is important to me and that is why I want to maintain it [*assertion of positive emotion*].'

Denise struggled through her assertion with Naomi. Her fears kept coming to the surface, and at one point Denise felt an urge to slip back into the pleasing role so as to gain Naomi's approval. By sticking to her assertion, though, Denise found she received more respect from Naomi. This gave Denise a new experience in her life, being genuine and true to herself and still receiving the approval of a close friend. Although life did present further challenges for Denise in relation to her assertion coaching, she worked at maintaining her new healthy philosophy.

Assertion coaching at work

The relationship with a work colleague is characterized by its formality, where interaction is more restricted. In other words, you are not constructing or maintaining a relationship that is intimate or which would resemble a close friendship. Not that you treat your colleagues as members of the public, or endeavour to keep yourself so far removed that you appear remote and cold. Rather, your loyalty is based on professional rather than emotional grounds, yet still maintaining a genuine concern for their welfare and progress. Again, maintaining appropriate boundaries with work colleagues is a delicate balance between formality and humanity.

Defining the boundaries between work colleagues and close friends was a real challenge for Colin. He would almost automatically attempt to forge an inappropriate close friendship with each member of his staff. He would then be devastated when he found out they were abusing his trust, or mocking him as 'weak' behind his back. In his assertion coaching sessions Colin learned that he was fostering this behaviour by not maintaining a good working relationship with his employees. Colin did exceptionally well at working on this and constructed the following healthy belief to underpin his healthy assertion:

'I would like to be a nice person with everybody, but this is neither necessary nor always possible.'

Holding this belief Colin implemented an appraisal system at work, which he explained sent out a clear message to his staff that he was 'large and in charge'. He then began following up debts that he had avoided through fear of the debtors not liking him. What follows is an interaction that Colin had with a business partner who was refusing to accept the fact that Colin's company owed him less money than he originally believed was owed him.

Colin: 'Thank you, Nick, for attending the meeting. I am concerned that you believe my company owes you £15,000 more than we actually do [*identified emotion*]. I have done my calculations and have presented them for you.'

This was a significant change in communication style. Previously Colin would use phrases like 'mate' as terms of endearment. This often indicated to the other person that he could be manipulated and pushed around.

Nick: 'No, these are not right. I know you owe that money.'

Colin: 'I have done my calculations [*repetition of Colin's specific point*]. Check them and if they are wrong I will amend them [*suggested compromise*].'

Nick: 'No, this is rubbish, you owe me that money.'

Colin: 'Nick, I can see you are getting annoyed [*reflecting Nick's emotion*]. Can you provide any evidence to prove it?'

Nick: 'I just know.'

Colin: 'That is not good enough. If you continue refusing to consider my calculations then I will not do business with you again, I will find another contractor [*three strikes technique*].'

This was real progress and actually spelled the end of Colin's assertion coaching sessions. Colin would have previously paid the money so as to avoid the confrontation and Nick's possible disapproval. Instead, Colin maintained in his mind that this relationship was professional and that he did not always have to be the 'nice person' to survive in life. The result was that Nick decided to do further business with Colin as he respected Colin's business practice.

Assertion coaching with members of the public

Courtesy is of the highest priority when asserting yourself with members of the public. Remember, everyone is equal, even if they are acting in a very inconsiderate way. Returning that inconsiderate behaviour with impolite assertion is not the answer, as you will then be condoning that level of behaviour. To equip you in being assertive with members of the public, we have taken the two most requested scenarios from our assertion coaching workshops. These are:

1 unsatisfactory treatment in the service industry, i.e. restaurant staff, retail outlets, staff on public transport;
2 inconsiderate behaviour in public places, i.e. smoking in non-smoking areas, being noisy in quieter public places, pushing ahead of others in queues.

The first scenario we will highlight is assertion with people who are in the service industry. We have chosen to use an example of assertion in a restaurant. The following is a common scenario rather than being a specific individual example:

You:	'Excuse me, waiter, I am really not happy with this meal, it is not what I was expecting [*identifying specific that you do not like*]. I would like to re-order from the menu, please [*suggested compromise*].'
Waiter:	'But it is what you ordered.'
You:	'Yes, it is what I ordered [*reflecting content*], but I am not happy with it [*repetition*]. I would like to re-order from the menu, please [*repetition of the suggested compromise*].'
Waiter:	'Perhaps you would like to explain what it is you do not like.'
You:	'I am disappointed with the service I am receiving from you [*identifying specific you do not like*]. If you continue not to hear me and not act on what I am asking, I will want to see your manager [*three strikes technique*].'
Waiter:	Shrugs shoulders in a nonchalant fashion.
You:	'I want to speak to your manager [*implementing the three strikes technique*].'
Manager:	'Yes, madam.'
You:	'[*full explanation*] I want a full refund or a replacement of my meal [*repetition of suggested compromise*].'

The above highlights how you can always seek higher assistance if you are dissatisfied with the service provided. On most occasions, requesting the individual's superior will, not surprisingly, evoke a better response. In actual fact, we suggest to our clients that if they have not asserted themselves before, then the service industry is a good place to start. We will discuss why this is so in the concluding chapter.

The second scenario we will now highlight is assertion with people who are encroaching on your civil liberties with their inconsiderate behaviour. We have chosen to use an example of assertion with a member of the public who is smoking in a non-smoking area. This is a common scenario and is not taken from a specific individual example. We have set it in a carriage on a train:

You: 'Excuse me, you may not have noticed but this is a non-smoking area.'

Smoker: 'Yes, I noticed. It is just one cigarette, it won't kill you.'

You: 'I appreciate it is just one cigarette [reflecting content]. I would be very grateful if you would put it out [suggested compromise].'

Smoker: 'No, I have been dying for this cigarette all day.'

You: 'I understand you are desperate for that cigarette [reflecting feeling]. If you do not put it out, though, I will report it at the next station [appropriate application of the three strikes technique]. I will also move carriage at the next stop and that will be quite an inconvenience for me.'

As you can see, politeness and courtesy are paramount with complete strangers. It is the aim of assertion with members of the public that you win them over rather than win your point. In our experience, appropriate assertion usually yields positive responses, as people are generally receptive to courtesy.

The point to remember is that, whether you are dealing with the service industry or with members of the public, nothing will change unless you assert yourself. Complaining in your head will not get your meal changed, and smarting at breathing in somebody else's smoke will not clear the air. More often than not you will have to pipe up politely to maintain a comfortable environment.

Summary

In this chapter we have given some specific real-life examples of assertion in particular areas of your life. They were in intimate relationships, with friends, with work colleagues and with members of the public. These are not scripts that you have to follow closely: word-perfect assertion does not exist. Rather, view them as templates, and copy the structure. You will then be able to make them fit to all the different scenarios life will throw your way. To illustrate; trying to copy these examples exactly is much like being given directions to a specific destination while travelling. They are useful for that journey only. It is not as helpful as being taught to read the map you are using. Once you have grasped how to read a map, understanding the referencing and format system, then you can go wherever you like. In effect, use this chapter as a map and integrate the format of asserting boundaries with the particular person with whom you wish to be assertive. We encourage you to avoid trying to copy the words: just make use of the structure.

In the concluding chapter we will consider how you can change your new-found knowledge into action. Assertion coaching may seem easy in theory but practice can be very challenging. In the final chapter we will help you capitalize on what you have learned. We will highlight a structured programme that will help you start and maintain your assertion.

8

How to implement and maintain your philosophy and practice of assertion

John found it very hard to drop his aggressive communication style. He had used his aggression time and again for many years to quickly motivate others to do exactly what he wanted. His aggression was an old communication habit that he found very hard to break. John failed a number of times to implement and then maintain his practice of assertion. He often started well but then reverted back to aggression.

Although behaving passively, Joan shared a similar experience. She found it hard to let go of her automatic desire to stay quiet when her husband put her down in the company of others. Joan explained that every fibre of her body was telling her to 'shut up' and 'just do what he asks'. Her passivity was an old communication habit that she maintained through her practice of it.

The way you used to communicate, be it aggressively or passively, will be as familiar to you as an old habit. You will need to imitate John and Joan's determination if you want to be healthily assertive and overcome your unhelpful aggression or passivity. It will seem far more comfortable to use your old way of communicating even though you may in principle believe that assertion is a better way for you to communicate. For this reason we will complete your assertion coaching with a chapter on how to implement and then maintain your assertion philosophy.

What is an assertion philosophy?

We believe that a good assertion philosophy helps you to initiate your assertion and then to maintain it. The philosophy of assertion is made up of the two following components. First, it involves you resolving in your mind and heart to act assertively even though you may be uncomfortable. Second, it involves you thinking about the other person before being assertive. This means that you maintain a balance between your own interests and those of the other person.

First, resolve in your mind to act assertively even though you may be uncomfortable. As stated at the beginning of this chapter your communication style, although unhelpful, 'feels' comfortable. It's tried and tested and you're used to it. That is why when you first attempt healthy assertion it is going to feel very uncomfortable, perhaps even scary. What will most probably happen is that as you think of being assertive your fear will start to well up. At this point your irrational self-talk will tell you to stop what you're doing and go back to the old way of communicating. It will seem as if every cell in your body is resisting this communication change. Do not give in! This natural tendency will need to be fought with all your intellectual and emotional might. Use determination and tolerate the discomfort. Then keep reminding yourself why you are doing it. Even though uncomfortable, you are doing it to liberate yourself from a way of communicating that has kept you enslaved for years. This is liberation time! When being assertive, reflect on the outcome for you as an individual: no longer will you be the doormat, or conversely the unkind dictator.

In summary, do not give in to discomfort and decide that assertion is not for you. Even when it seems that every fibre of your being is telling you otherwise, stick to your healthy resolve by reflecting on the positive outcome for you as a person. This is the first of the two components to your assertion philosophy.

The second component is that you think about the other person before being assertive. This means that you maintain a balance between your own interests and those of the other person. As we have already stated, equality is at the heart of assertion. For this reason it will be rare that you get exactly what you want all the time without some form of compromise. If you hold to the idea that your assertion must give you the ideal outcome you will not practise assertion for very long. Rather, you will resort to aggression. For this reason be decent in your application of assertion. It will not be necessary for you to be assertive about everything you do not like. Temper your decision to be assertive with fairness. To do this, ask yourself, 'Am I expecting perfection from others, or does their behaviour warrant assertion?' and 'Am I just pursuing my own preference or pleasure, and disregarding others?'

We are not encouraging you to talk yourself out of being assertive when something is not good enough. This will keep you passive. Nor are we encouraging that you jump on every little thing that does not seem to be going your way. This is too egotistical and promotes a self-absorbed philosophy that will leave you unfulfilled and dissatisfied in your relationships. The reason for this is that it will seem that everyone lets you down, when in reality it is your high ideals that are letting you down. What we are encouraging is that you accept that perfect satisfaction in relationships is an unattainable goal. This means finding a balance between pleasing yourself and considering the other person.

In summary, we encourage you not to give up being assertive, even though you will probably feel very uncomfortable at first. Your discomfort will not kill you, and it will subside the more you are assertive. Above all, stop yourself from running away from assertion, as this will only serve to make it harder the next time you attempt it.

Remember also that you are striving for equality, not supremacy. Be content with a reasonable degree of satisfaction in your relationships, not demanding it all goes your way all of the time.

We encourage that you consider the above and then devise your own assertion philosophy that you can practise before, during and after being assertive. Colin did this, putting the two components into his own words. It read as follows:

'I resolve that I will stand up for what I believe in, not relinquishing personal preference to just go along with the crowd. I will temper my assertion with decency by striving for a reasonable degree of satisfaction in all my relationships. My goal is to be content with a "good enough" living environment and not to be assertive unnecessarily.'

Colin encapsulates well the main tenets of our assertion philosophy. We will now highlight how to start being assertive.

How to start

To get started, think small rather than big. We regularly encourage our clients to start with small challenging tasks at first. This means, for instance, that if your mother is the greatest bane of your life, proving to be very stubborn and cantankerous in her later years, it may not be a good idea to start practising your assertion with her first. Set yourself a realistic task in order to get practice. The reason we encourage thinking small and being realistic is that we have found that those individuals who aim high at first can feel very overwhelmed by assertion. They leap in, tackling a difficult candidate first off, trying to apply all their new learning in one fell swoop. Lacking practice, their assertion does not go as planned; this acts as a discouragement for them. In fact, in a few cases it has reinforced the false idea that they are just not cut out to stand up for themselves. For this reason we recommend aiming realistically low initially, with small bite-size assertion tasks at first.

Just how do you do this?

First, think about the people you would find most challenging to be assertive with, and write their names at the top of Table 8.1 ('My assertion action plan'). In the outer margin, rate how challenging you believe, at present, it would be to be assertive with that person. The scale is 0–100 per cent, 0 representing no challenge at all, and 100 per cent representing extremely challenging. We have also added an extra column for the proposed date of each of your assertion tasks. This will aid you in keeping on schedule so that you do not allow time to slip by without being assertive.

Second, think who would be the least challenging person to be assertive with. Add their name to the bottom of the list. Now, work your way up the list, from the bottom up, progressively making each assertion assignment more challenging, until you reach your most challenging assignment.

Who to start with? Initially we encourage our clients to aim at the service industry. Believe it or not, they are paid to be polite, so this provides a good training ground. Again, it does not have to be big at first. Denise started with asserting herself with children, then moving on to shop assistants; Colin started with a delivery driver who delivered to his place of business. Be realistic in order to get the most from your early attempts at assertion. We encourage you to seize the moment and start making your list now using Table 8.1. If you are having difficulty devising your own list you can refer to Table 8.2, which was Denise's proposed action plan.

Table 8.1 My assertion action plan

Name of person I am going to be assertive with	Challenge 0–100%	Proposed date
1. (Most challenging)		
2.		
3.		
4.		
5.		
6.		
7.		
8.		
9.		
10. (Least challenging)		

Table 8.2 Denise's assertion action plan

Name of person I am going to be assertive with	Challenge 0–100%	Proposed date
1. (Most challenging) Asserting myself with Mother about the way she treated my sister and me in our childhood.	100	One month
2. Asserting myself with Anne (sister) about the way she has treated Mother and me over the last three years.	85	One month
3. Asserting myself with Fred (husband) about the way he takes me for granted at times.	79	Three weeks
4. Asking daughter not to ring me for reassurance so often.	65	Three weeks
5. Asserting myself with family about always being the one who hosts weekly family meal.	62	End of next week
6. Asserting myself with Naomi following Saturday's missed meal engagement.	50	Next week
7. Saying 'no' to friend when asked to babysit her children.	48	Next week
8. Returning meal at restaurant when eating with friends.	48	Weekend
9. Returning garment and asking for money back from sales assistant.	40	Weekend
10. (Least challenging) Saying 'no' to the young child my daughter nannies for.	20	Tomorrow

As we are sure you have noticed, each task Denise takes on challenges her assertion skills progressively more. This is a good example of how to get started. Small steps taken in quick succession will aid you in covering distance quickly and thoroughly. You may also have noticed that some of Denise's assignments were scheduled very close together. We encourage you to do the same – keep striking while the iron is hot! Allowing too much time to elapse will make each assignment seem more difficult than it actually is. You will find it hard at times and this may erode your initial enthusiasm for assertion. This is why we will finish your assertion coaching with top tips on maintaining your resolve.

How to maintain your resolve

It is one thing to start a race; it is another to finish it as a winner. To be a winner in assertion coaching you will need to maintain a high tolerance to discomfort and frustration. The reason for this is that assertion is temporarily the more difficult option. Assertion requires more effort initially and you may reason that it is far easier just to leave the situation, hoping it will sort itself out. In addition to this it can be frustrating when you observe that your assertion may not have made a lasting difference in the behaviour of those you were being assertive with. When experiencing this discomfort and frustration you may start to become indifferent about maintaining your new assertive behaviour. This is the time to keep up your resolve by reasoning on the following points.

The ability to withstand hardship and continue to perform, especially when uncomfortable, will give you stamina, courage and strength. If you remain assertive instead of fleeing or giving up, you break the shackles in your mind that have enslaved and ensnared you. This higher tolerance to discomfort is the quality that keeps you on your feet with your face to the wind. It is the virtue that can transmute the hardest trial into success, because beyond the temporary pain you see the goal. One of the main goals enhancing your personal development of assertion, this brings confidence and aids you in seeing other important projects through to their completion. This is where you gain the greatest reward.

Those who maintain their resolve to be assertive finally reach their objective; these are the happy, liberated ones. Those who give in to the discomfort and drop out may get some temporary relief by avoiding the immediate responsibility and pressure. Yet they create an atmosphere of unhappiness for themselves; by giving in to the discomfort they experience a loss of confidence and a lack of self-respect, and wrongly assume that they are a complete failure. When your assertive resolve weakens, ask yourself: how do I want my life to turn out? Do I want to give in to this temporary discomfort and lose confidence in myself, or do I want to build my self-confidence up and gain strength of character? Finally, on this point consider our make-up. It is an inherent desire for us to want to accomplish something in our lives. There is nothing that can take the place of the exhilarating joy of accomplishment when you stick to your resolve and continue to be assertive.

How can you maintain your resolve even when your assertion does not seem to be making much lasting difference in the behaviour of those around you? This was the very obstacle that undermined George's determination. George almost gave up after the first hurdle as he realized that his father would have a natural tendency to slide back to the old way of acting. This fuelled frustration for George, but he decided to tolerate the temporary frustration and persist in his assertion. He accepted that there rarely is an immediate change in the behaviour from others following initial attempts at assertion. This frustrated George, as he did not want it to be that hard; he thought one dose of his assertion would move his father on for good. His assumption was misplaced, so to encourage him to continue with his assertion we considered the alternative. The alternative was to go back to living a life where he attempted to prove himself instead of enjoying himself. If he returned to that way of living he would once again need to hone the skill of second-guessing what everyone else expected him to say or do. George decided that giving up assertion was a higher price to pay than accepting the frustration of having to persist time and again with his father.

To summarize, when you have a moment of indifference and your resolve is low, focus on the future gain, not the temporary pain. Give in to the temporary discomfort and you will be nurturing a defeatist attitude that will feed into a lack of self-confidence and low self-respect. In addition, if it seems that you are not getting any immediate change from people around you, keep persisting. Reflect on the alternative to being assertive. Then consider how liberated you will be if you persist in your assertion.

Summary and conclusion

In this chapter we have highlighted how to construct an assertion philosophy. Your assertion philosophy will preferably encapsulate the idea of not giving in to discomfort, but also not asserting yourself on every little thing that you do not like as this is unhealthy. In addition we showed the steps that can get you started in your assertion. Drawing up an action plan (Table 8.1) and aiming low initially is the recipe for a successful outcome in beginning your assertion. We have also highlighted how to maintain your resolve to be assertive. By focusing on the long-term gain and not giving in to the temporary discomfort and frustration you will remain on course with your assertion coaching.

In conclusion, assertion will liberate you and help you to create a peaceful satisfying environment in which it will be a pleasure for you to live. This will require some temporary pain, but true assertion pays dividends almost immediately. It teaches others how you wish to be treated. In addition to this, assertion stops you having regrets in life, as you are not left wishing you had said or done something long after the event has passed. Assertion also fosters courage, the quality that drives you to do what you want to do despite feeling fear. Do not shrink back from being assertive through the dread of others hurting. Stop yourself from taking responsibility for the feelings of others to the detriment of your own. Your feelings are just as important as everyone else's!

We encourage you to seize the moment right now. Do not wait until you feel confident – that time will come after some practice. Start your assertion today. Just go for it. We believe it will add colour to your relationships and give you a sense of confidence that will pervade everything you do. We sincerely thank you for giving us the opportunity of imparting these new skills to you. We are strong advocates of assertion over passivity and aggression. We also want to let you know that we practise these skills every day – sometimes with success and other times not so successfully, but we accept our fallibility. We are sure that, applied accurately, they will give you the satisfying life you desire. We wish you the very best in your endeavours.

Index

ABC framework: identifying passivity 28–30; REBT and 23–4

advice: manipulative 18; prescriptive 72

aggression: asserting positive emotions 83–4; characteristics of 4–6; communicating needs/desires 46–8; contrasted with assertion 9–11; identifying 16–20; over-compensation 11–12; using ABC framework 25–8

agreement/disagreement: identifying 63; requests for specific examples and 73–5, 79

anger: discomfort 26; ego 26; unhealthy 25–7

apologies 84–5

assertion: agreement and requests for specific examples 73–5, 79; beliefs and 30–1; benefits of 111–12; breaking old habits 1; contrasted with aggression and passivity 8–11; definition and nature of 3–4; focus and repetition 66–7; in friendships 98–100; healthy boundaries 88–91; identifying behaviour 11–16; in intimate relationships 95–8; keeping the balance 106–7; maintaining resolve 110–11; negotiating a compromise 77–8, 79; planning action 107–9; preparing your case 62–6, 79; with public 101–3; sticking to resolve 105–6; structures of 103–4; using discretion and tact 85–7

awfulizing: beliefs and 54–5; non-56–7

beliefs 60–1; ABC framework and 23–5; aggression and 25–8; in an easy life 48–9; awfulizing 27, 29; communicating needs/desires 46–8; forceful healthy self-statements 58–9; frustration tolerance 27–8, 29, 31; healthy and unhealthy 52–4; non-awfulizing 30–1; passivity and 28–30; questioning your own 52–8; rational-emotive imagery (REI) 58, 59–60; rigid and demanding 27; underpinning assertion 30–1

blame: aggression and 5

body language 11; aggression 118–20; assertive 15–16; listening skills 67–8; passivity 23–4

boundaries: healthy 88–91

bullying 4

Colin: acting sincerely 36–7; asserting emotions 87; introduction to 2; keeping his resolve 107; negotiating a compromise 77–8; passivity 7; using ABC framework 28–30; workplace assertion 100–1

communication: breaking old habits 1; changing the subject 73; competitive and to the point 92–3; considerate and selfless 93–4; defence triggers 70–3, 79; of feelings 49–51; listening skills 67–70, 79; of needs/desires 46–8; negative and critical 93; open and chatty 92; precise and detailed 92;